50 Cooking with Craft Beer Recipes for Home

By: Kelly Johnson

Table of Contents

- Beer-Battered Onion Rings
- Stout and Cheddar Soup
- Beer and Honey Glazed Chicken Wings
- IPA Macaroni and Cheese
- Beer-Braised Bratwurst
- Belgian Ale Mussels
- Beer and Pretzel Caramel Brownies
- Hefeweizen Battered Fish Tacos
- Beer and Bacon Potato Salad
- Porter Braised Short Ribs
- Pale Ale Marinated Grilled Chicken
- Beer Cheese Dip
- Pumpkin Ale Risotto
- Beer-Braised Pork Belly
- Honey Ale Glazed Salmon
- Guinness Chocolate Cake
- Beer and Mustard Glazed Ham
- IPA Pickled Vegetables
- Beer and Sriracha Shrimp Skewers
- Saison Poached Pears
- Beer and Garlic Roasted Potatoes
- Lager-Battered Shrimp Po' Boy
- Beer and Maple Glazed Carrots
- Double IPA Barbecue Sauce
- Beer-Braised Beef Stew
- Pumpkin Ale Cheesecake
- Stout and Coffee BBQ Ribs
- Beer and Cheddar Bread
- Ale-Braised Sausages with Peppers and Onions
- Beer and Rosemary Focaccia
- Honey Ale Glazed Brussels Sprouts

- Beer and Dijon Mustard Chicken Thighs
- IPA Citrus Sorbet
- Beer-Battered Avocado Fries
- Beer and Honey Glazed Roasted Nuts
- Pale Ale Lemon Bars
- Beer and Chipotle Pulled Pork
- Guinness Beef Chili
- Beer and Basil Grilled Corn on the Cob
- Beer-Braised Chicken Tacos
- Brown Ale and Mushroom Risotto
- IPA Ceviche
- Beer and Herb Marinated Grilled Vegetables
- Beer and Caramelized Onion Pizza
- Chocolate Stout Pudding
- Beer and Lime Grilled Shrimp
- Ale and Garlic Roasted Chicken
- IPA Pineapple Salsa
- Beer and Sage Butter Pasta
- Porter and Chocolate Mousse

Beer-Battered Onion Rings

Ingredients:

- 2 large onions, cut into rings
- 1 1/2 cups all-purpose flour
- 1 teaspoon baking powder
- 1/2 teaspoon salt
- 1/4 teaspoon black pepper
- 1 1/4 cups cold craft beer (choose a light ale or lager)
- Vegetable oil, for frying

Instructions:

In a large mixing bowl, whisk together the flour, baking powder, salt, and black pepper.

Gradually pour in the cold beer, whisking continuously to avoid lumps. The batter should have a smooth consistency.

Let the batter rest for about 15-20 minutes. This allows the beer to react with the other ingredients and gives the batter a lighter texture.

Heat vegetable oil in a deep fryer or a large, deep pan to 375°F (190°C).

Dip each onion ring into the batter, ensuring it is well-coated, and let any excess batter drip off.

Carefully place the battered onion rings into the hot oil, a few at a time, making sure not to overcrowd the pan.

Fry the onion rings for 2-3 minutes on each side or until they turn golden brown and crispy.

Use a slotted spoon to remove the onion rings from the oil and place them on a paper towel-lined plate to absorb excess oil.

Sprinkle with a little extra salt while they're still hot.

Serve immediately and enjoy your homemade beer-battered onion rings as a tasty appetizer or side dish. They pair perfectly with your favorite dipping sauce, such as aioli or spicy ketchup.

Stout and Cheddar Soup

Ingredients:

- 1/4 cup unsalted butter
- 1 onion, diced
- 2 carrots, peeled and diced
- 2 celery stalks, diced
- 3 cloves garlic, minced
- 1/3 cup all-purpose flour
- 2 cups chicken or vegetable broth
- 1 1/2 cups stout beer (e.g., Guinness)
- 3 cups whole milk
- 3 cups sharp cheddar cheese, shredded
- Salt and pepper, to taste
- Optional toppings: chopped green onions, crispy bacon bits

Instructions:

In a large pot, melt the butter over medium heat. Add the diced onion, carrots, and celery. Cook until the vegetables are softened, about 5-7 minutes.
Add the minced garlic and cook for an additional 1-2 minutes until fragrant.
Sprinkle the flour over the vegetables and stir to combine, creating a roux. Cook for 2-3 minutes to eliminate the raw flour taste.
Slowly whisk in the chicken or vegetable broth, making sure to eliminate any lumps. Then, pour in the stout beer and milk, stirring continuously to combine.
Bring the soup to a simmer, stirring occasionally, and let it cook for about 10-15 minutes until it thickens.
Reduce the heat to low, and gradually add the shredded cheddar cheese, stirring until the cheese is melted and the soup is smooth.
Season the soup with salt and pepper to taste. Keep in mind that the cheese is salty, so adjust accordingly.
Continue to simmer for an additional 5-10 minutes to allow the flavors to meld together.
Ladle the Stout and Cheddar Soup into bowls and garnish with chopped green onions or crispy bacon bits if desired.
Serve the soup hot, and enjoy the comforting combination of stout and cheddar flavors. This soup pairs well with crusty bread or a side salad.

Beer and Honey Glazed Chicken Wings

Ingredients:

- 2 lbs chicken wings, split at joints, tips discarded
- Salt and black pepper, to taste
- 1 cup beer (choose a light ale or lager)
- 1/2 cup honey
- 1/4 cup soy sauce
- 2 tablespoons Dijon mustard
- 2 cloves garlic, minced
- 1 teaspoon smoked paprika
- 1/2 teaspoon onion powder
- 1/4 teaspoon cayenne pepper (optional, for heat)
- Sesame seeds and chopped green onions for garnish

Instructions:

Preheat your oven to 400°F (200°C).
Pat the chicken wings dry with paper towels and season with salt and black pepper.
Place the wings on a baking sheet lined with parchment paper or aluminum foil, ensuring they are spread out in a single layer.
Bake the wings in the preheated oven for 45-50 minutes or until they are golden brown and crispy.
While the wings are baking, prepare the beer and honey glaze. In a saucepan over medium heat, combine the beer, honey, soy sauce, Dijon mustard, minced garlic, smoked paprika, onion powder, and cayenne pepper (if using).
Bring the mixture to a simmer, then reduce the heat and let it simmer for 15-20 minutes, or until the glaze thickens slightly. Stir occasionally.
Once the wings are cooked, transfer them to a large bowl.
Pour the beer and honey glaze over the wings and toss until they are evenly coated.
Return the glazed wings to the baking sheet and bake for an additional 10-15 minutes, allowing the glaze to caramelize and create a sticky coating.
Remove the wings from the oven, sprinkle with sesame seeds and chopped green onions for garnish.
Serve the beer and honey glazed chicken wings hot as an appetizer or main dish.
Enjoy the sweet and savory flavors with your favorite dipping sauce on the side.

IPA Macaroni and Cheese

Ingredients:

- 8 oz elbow macaroni or your favorite pasta
- 1/4 cup unsalted butter
- 1/4 cup all-purpose flour
- 2 cups whole milk
- 1 cup India Pale Ale (IPA)
- 3 cups sharp cheddar cheese, shredded
- 1 cup Gruyere cheese, shredded
- 1/2 teaspoon Dijon mustard
- 1/2 teaspoon garlic powder
- Salt and black pepper, to taste
- 1/2 cup breadcrumbs (optional, for topping)
- Chopped fresh parsley for garnish

Instructions:

Preheat your oven to 350°F (175°C) and grease a baking dish.
Cook the macaroni according to the package instructions until al dente. Drain and set aside.
In a large saucepan, melt the butter over medium heat. Add the flour and whisk continuously for 2-3 minutes to create a roux.
Gradually pour in the milk, whisking constantly to avoid lumps. Continue whisking until the mixture thickens.
Slowly add the IPA to the saucepan, stirring continuously. Allow the mixture to simmer for 2-3 minutes, letting the alcohol cook off.
Reduce the heat to low and add the shredded cheddar and Gruyere cheeses to the sauce. Stir until the cheese is fully melted and the sauce is smooth.
Stir in the Dijon mustard, garlic powder, salt, and black pepper to taste.
Add the cooked macaroni to the cheese sauce, tossing to coat the pasta evenly.
If desired, transfer the macaroni and cheese to the greased baking dish. Sprinkle breadcrumbs over the top for a crunchy crust.
Bake in the preheated oven for 20-25 minutes, or until the top is golden and the cheese is bubbly.
Remove from the oven, garnish with chopped parsley, and let it cool for a few minutes before serving.

Serve the IPA Macaroni and Cheese hot, savoring the rich and hoppy flavors from the IPA along with the creamy cheese sauce. Enjoy this elevated take on a classic dish!

Beer-Braised Bratwurst

Ingredients:

- 4 bratwurst sausages
- 2 tablespoons vegetable oil
- 1 large onion, thinly sliced
- 2 cloves garlic, minced
- 1 bottle of your favorite beer (pale ale, lager, or bock work well)
- 1 cup chicken or beef broth
- 2 tablespoons Dijon mustard
- 1 teaspoon caraway seeds (optional)
- Salt and black pepper, to taste
- Fresh parsley, chopped (for garnish)
- Mustard and sauerkraut (for serving)

Instructions:

In a large skillet or Dutch oven, heat the vegetable oil over medium-high heat. Add the bratwurst sausages to the skillet and brown them on all sides, about 5 minutes. Remove them from the skillet and set aside.

In the same skillet, add the sliced onions and cook until they become soft and translucent, about 5 minutes.

Add the minced garlic and cook for an additional 1-2 minutes until fragrant.

Pour in the beer and broth, scraping the bottom of the skillet to release any flavorful bits. Bring the mixture to a simmer.

Stir in the Dijon mustard and caraway seeds (if using). Season with salt and black pepper to taste.

Return the browned bratwurst sausages to the skillet, ensuring they are submerged in the liquid.

Reduce the heat to low, cover the skillet, and let the bratwurst simmer in the beer mixture for 20-25 minutes.

Once the bratwurst is cooked through, remove them from the skillet and set aside.

Increase the heat to medium-high and let the beer mixture simmer and reduce for an additional 10-15 minutes until it thickens.

Serve the beer-braised bratwurst over a bed of sauerkraut, spooning the reduced beer sauce over the top.

Garnish with chopped fresh parsley and serve with mustard on the side. Enjoy your beer-braised bratwurst with a side of crusty bread or potatoes, soaking up the delicious beer-infused flavors.

Belgian Ale Mussels

Ingredients:

- 2 lbs fresh mussels, cleaned and debearded
- 2 tablespoons unsalted butter
- 1 tablespoon olive oil
- 1 onion, finely chopped
- 2 cloves garlic, minced
- 1 celery stalk, finely chopped
- 1 carrot, peeled and finely chopped
- 1 cup Belgian ale (such as a Tripel or Witbier)
- 1/2 cup chicken or vegetable broth
- 1 bay leaf
- 1 teaspoon Dijon mustard
- Salt and black pepper, to taste
- Fresh parsley, chopped (for garnish)
- Crusty bread (for serving)

Instructions:

In a large pot or Dutch oven, melt the butter and olive oil over medium heat.
Add the chopped onion, garlic, celery, and carrot to the pot. Cook until the vegetables are softened, about 5 minutes.
Pour in the Belgian ale and chicken or vegetable broth. Add the bay leaf, Dijon mustard, salt, and black pepper. Stir to combine.
Bring the liquid to a simmer and let it cook for 5-7 minutes, allowing the flavors to meld.
Add the cleaned mussels to the pot, making sure they are well-distributed. Cover the pot with a lid.
Steam the mussels for 5-7 minutes, or until they have opened. Discard any mussels that do not open.
Using a slotted spoon, transfer the mussels to serving bowls.
Strain the cooking liquid to remove any sand or debris and pour it over the mussels.
Garnish with chopped fresh parsley.
Serve the Belgian Ale Mussels hot with crusty bread on the side for soaking up the flavorful broth.

Enjoy this delightful dish that combines the sweetness of mussels with the aromatic and slightly fruity notes of Belgian ale. It's perfect for a cozy and satisfying meal.

Beer and Pretzel Caramel Brownies

Ingredients:

For the Brownies:

- 1 cup unsalted butter
- 2 cups granulated sugar
- 4 large eggs
- 1 teaspoon vanilla extract
- 1/2 cup cocoa powder
- 1/2 teaspoon salt
- 1 cup all-purpose flour

For the Pretzel Caramel Topping:

- 1 cup soft pretzels, crushed
- 1 cup caramel sauce (store-bought or homemade)
- 1/4 cup beer (choose a malty beer like a stout or porter)
- Sea salt for sprinkling

Instructions:

Preheat the oven:

Preheat your oven to 350°F (175°C). Grease and line a 9x13-inch baking pan with parchment paper.

Make the Brownie Batter:

In a saucepan, melt the butter over medium heat. Remove from heat and stir in the sugar until well combined. Add the eggs one at a time, beating well after each addition. Stir in the vanilla extract. Sift in the cocoa powder and salt, and then fold in the flour until just combined.

Bake the Brownies:

Pour the brownie batter into the prepared baking pan and spread it evenly. Bake in the preheated oven for 25-30 minutes or until a toothpick inserted into the center comes out with moist crumbs (not wet batter). Remove from the oven and let the brownies cool in the pan.

Prepare the Pretzel Caramel Topping:

In a small saucepan, heat the caramel sauce and beer over low heat, stirring until well combined and warmed through. Remove from heat.

Add Pretzel Topping:

Sprinkle the crushed pretzels over the cooled brownies. Pour the warm caramel-beer sauce evenly over the pretzels. Use a spatula to spread it evenly.

Set and Cut:

Allow the brownies to set at room temperature or in the refrigerator until the caramel is firm. Once set, lift the brownies from the pan using the parchment paper and place them on a cutting board. Sprinkle with sea salt.

Cut and Serve:

Cut the brownies into squares or rectangles. Serve and enjoy these decadent beer and pretzel caramel brownies!

These brownies are a delightful combination of sweet, salty, and malty flavors that make them a unique and delicious treat for any occasion.

Hefeweizen Battered Fish Tacos

Ingredients:

For the Hefeweizen Battered Fish:

- 1 lb white fish fillets (such as cod or tilapia), cut into strips
- 1 cup all-purpose flour
- 1 teaspoon baking powder
- 1/2 teaspoon salt
- 1 cup Hefeweizen beer
- Vegetable oil for frying

For the Slaw:

- 2 cups cabbage, thinly shredded
- 1 carrot, julienned
- 1/4 cup mayonnaise
- 1 tablespoon apple cider vinegar
- 1 teaspoon honey
- Salt and pepper, to taste

For Assembling Tacos:

- Flour or corn tortillas
- Fresh cilantro, chopped
- Lime wedges

Instructions:

Prepare the Slaw:

In a bowl, combine shredded cabbage and julienned carrot. In a separate small bowl, whisk together mayonnaise, apple cider vinegar, honey, salt, and pepper. Pour the dressing over the cabbage and carrot mixture, tossing until well coated. Refrigerate the slaw while preparing the rest of the ingredients.
Make the Hefeweizen Battered Fish:

- In a large mixing bowl, whisk together the flour, baking powder, and salt.
- Gradually add the Hefeweizen beer, whisking continuously until you have a smooth batter.
- Heat vegetable oil in a deep fryer or a large, deep pan to 375°F (190°C).
- Dip each fish strip into the batter, ensuring it is well-coated, and carefully place it into the hot oil.
- Fry the fish for 3-4 minutes on each side or until golden brown and crispy. Remove with a slotted spoon and place on a paper towel-lined plate to absorb excess oil.

Assemble the Tacos:
- Warm the tortillas in a dry skillet or microwave.
- Place a couple of hefeweizen-battered fish strips on each tortilla.
- Top with a generous spoonful of the prepared slaw.
- Garnish with chopped cilantro and serve with lime wedges on the side.

Serve and Enjoy:

Serve the Hefeweizen Battered Fish Tacos immediately. Squeeze fresh lime juice over the top before enjoying.

These tacos offer a perfect balance of crispy fish, creamy slaw, and fresh toppings.

Enjoy the combination of flavors and textures in each delicious bite!

Beer and Bacon Potato Salad

Ingredients:

- 2 lbs red or Yukon Gold potatoes, washed and diced
- 1 cup beer (choose a light ale or lager)
- 1/2 cup mayonnaise
- 2 tablespoons Dijon mustard
- 1 tablespoon apple cider vinegar
- Salt and black pepper, to taste
- 6 slices bacon, cooked and crumbled
- 1/2 cup green onions, thinly sliced
- 1/4 cup fresh parsley, chopped
- 3 hard-boiled eggs, chopped (optional)

Instructions:

Boil the Potatoes:
- Place the diced potatoes in a large pot and cover them with cold water.
- Add a pinch of salt to the water and bring it to a boil.
- Simmer the potatoes for 10-15 minutes or until they are fork-tender. Be careful not to overcook; you want them firm for the salad.
- Drain the potatoes and let them cool to room temperature.

Prepare the Dressing:
- In a small saucepan, heat the beer over medium heat until it reduces by half. Allow it to cool.
- In a large bowl, whisk together the mayonnaise, Dijon mustard, apple cider vinegar, cooled beer, salt, and black pepper. Adjust the seasoning to taste.

Assemble the Potato Salad:
- Add the cooled diced potatoes to the dressing and gently toss until well coated.

Add Bacon and Other Ingredients:
- Fold in the crumbled bacon, sliced green onions, chopped parsley, and hard-boiled eggs (if using).

Chill and Serve:
- Refrigerate the potato salad for at least 2 hours to allow the flavors to meld.

Garnish and Serve:

- Before serving, garnish the potato salad with additional bacon, green onions, and parsley if desired.

Serve Cold:
- Serve the Beer and Bacon Potato Salad cold as a side dish at picnics, barbecues, or alongside grilled meats.

This potato salad combines the smoky richness of bacon with the subtle flavor of beer, creating a delicious and satisfying side dish that's perfect for various occasions. Enjoy!

Porter Braised Short Ribs

Ingredients:

- 4 lbs beef short ribs
- Salt and black pepper, to taste
- 2 tablespoons vegetable oil
- 1 large onion, diced
- 2 carrots, diced
- 3 cloves garlic, minced
- 2 tablespoons all-purpose flour
- 2 cups porter beer
- 1 cup beef broth
- 2 tablespoons tomato paste
- 1 tablespoon Worcestershire sauce
- 2 sprigs fresh thyme
- 2 bay leaves
- Mashed potatoes or creamy polenta, for serving
- Chopped fresh parsley, for garnish

Instructions:

Preheat the Oven:

Preheat your oven to 325°F (163°C).

Season the Short Ribs:

Season the short ribs with salt and black pepper.
Brown the Short Ribs:
- In a large oven-safe pot or Dutch oven, heat the vegetable oil over medium-high heat.
- Brown the short ribs on all sides, working in batches if necessary. Remove the ribs and set them aside.

Sauté Vegetables:
- In the same pot, add diced onion and carrots. Sauté until the vegetables are softened, about 5 minutes.
- Add minced garlic and sauté for an additional 1-2 minutes.

Create Roux:

- Sprinkle the flour over the vegetables and stir to create a roux. Cook for 2-3 minutes to eliminate the raw flour taste.

Add Liquid Ingredients:
- Pour in the porter beer, beef broth, tomato paste, and Worcestershire sauce. Stir well to combine.

Braise Short Ribs:
- Return the browned short ribs to the pot. Add fresh thyme and bay leaves.
- Bring the liquid to a simmer, then cover the pot with a lid.

Transfer to Oven:
- Transfer the pot to the preheated oven and braise for 2.5 to 3 hours or until the short ribs are fork-tender.

Serve:
- Remove the pot from the oven and discard the thyme sprigs and bay leaves.
- Serve the porter-braised short ribs over mashed potatoes or creamy polenta.
- Garnish with chopped fresh parsley.

Enjoy:
- Serve hot and enjoy the rich and savory flavors of porter-braised short ribs.

This hearty and flavorful dish is perfect for a special occasion or a cozy family dinner. The slow braising in porter beer results in tender and succulent short ribs with a robust and complex taste.

Pale Ale Marinated Grilled Chicken

Ingredients:

- 4 boneless, skinless chicken breasts or thighs
- 1 cup pale ale (choose your favorite brand)
- 1/4 cup olive oil
- 2 cloves garlic, minced
- 1 tablespoon Dijon mustard
- 1 tablespoon honey
- 1 teaspoon dried thyme
- 1 teaspoon smoked paprika
- Salt and black pepper, to taste
- Fresh parsley, chopped (for garnish)

Instructions:

Prepare the Marinade:

In a bowl, whisk together pale ale, olive oil, minced garlic, Dijon mustard, honey, dried thyme, smoked paprika, salt, and black pepper.

Marinate the Chicken:
- Place the chicken breasts or thighs in a resealable plastic bag or a shallow dish.
- Pour the pale ale marinade over the chicken, ensuring it is well-coated.
- Seal the bag or cover the dish with plastic wrap and marinate in the refrigerator for at least 2 hours, preferably longer for more flavor. Overnight marination is ideal.

Preheat the Grill:

Preheat your grill to medium-high heat.

Grill the Chicken:
- Remove the chicken from the marinade and let any excess drip off.
- Grill the chicken for about 6-8 minutes per side, or until the internal temperature reaches 165°F (74°C) and the chicken is cooked through.
- Baste the chicken with additional marinade during grilling for extra flavor.

Rest and Garnish:

- Once cooked, let the chicken rest for a few minutes before serving.
- Garnish with chopped fresh parsley for a burst of color and freshness.

Serve:

Serve the Pale Ale Marinated Grilled Chicken hot with your favorite side dishes, such as grilled vegetables, rice, or a crisp salad.

This marinated grilled chicken captures the essence of the pale ale, creating a flavorful and juicy dish with a hint of beer-inspired goodness. Enjoy the delicious results of this simple and tasty recipe!

Beer Cheese Dip

Ingredients:

- 2 cups sharp cheddar cheese, shredded
- 1 cup mozzarella cheese, shredded
- 1/2 cup cream cheese, softened
- 1 cup beer (choose a flavorful beer like an ale or lager)
- 2 cloves garlic, minced
- 1 teaspoon Dijon mustard
- 1/2 teaspoon Worcestershire sauce
- 1/2 teaspoon onion powder
- 1/4 teaspoon cayenne pepper (optional, for heat)
- Salt and black pepper, to taste
- 2 tablespoons all-purpose flour (optional, for thickening)
- Chopped fresh parsley or green onions for garnish (optional)

Instructions:

Prepare the Cheese:
- In a large mixing bowl, combine the sharp cheddar, mozzarella, and softened cream cheese.

Warm the Beer:
- In a saucepan over medium heat, warm the beer. You don't need to bring it to a boil; just heat it until it's warm to the touch.

Make the Cheese Mixture:
- Gradually add the warm beer to the cheese mixture, stirring continuously until the cheeses are melted and smooth.

Add Flavor and Seasonings:
- Stir in the minced garlic, Dijon mustard, Worcestershire sauce, onion powder, cayenne pepper (if using), salt, and black pepper. Mix well to combine.

Thicken (Optional):
- If you desire a thicker consistency, you can mix 2 tablespoons of all-purpose flour with a little water to make a paste. Stir the paste into the cheese mixture and continue to heat until thickened.

Serve:

- Once the dip reaches your desired consistency, transfer it to a serving bowl.

Garnish:
- Garnish with chopped fresh parsley or green onions for a burst of color and added flavor.

Serve Warm:
- Serve the Beer Cheese Dip warm with pretzels, tortilla chips, sliced baguette, or your favorite dipping items.

This Beer Cheese Dip is perfect for parties, game nights, or any gathering where you want to enjoy a tasty and comforting appetizer. The combination of beer and cheese creates a flavorful dip that's sure to be a hit!

Pumpkin Ale Risotto

Ingredients:

- 1 cup Arborio rice
- 1/2 cup pumpkin puree
- 1/2 cup dry white wine
- 3 cups chicken or vegetable broth, kept warm
- 1 cup pumpkin ale
- 1 small onion, finely chopped
- 2 cloves garlic, minced
- 1/2 cup Parmesan cheese, grated
- 2 tablespoons unsalted butter
- 2 tablespoons olive oil
- 1/2 teaspoon ground nutmeg
- Salt and black pepper, to taste
- Chopped fresh parsley for garnish

Instructions:

Prepare the Pumpkin Ale Mixture:
- In a saucepan, combine the pumpkin puree, pumpkin ale, and chicken or vegetable broth. Warm the mixture over low heat, keeping it at a simmer.

Sauté the Aromatics:
- In a large, heavy-bottomed pot or Dutch oven, heat the olive oil and 1 tablespoon of butter over medium heat.
- Add the finely chopped onion and cook until it becomes translucent, about 3-4 minutes.
- Stir in the minced garlic and cook for an additional 1-2 minutes until fragrant.

Toast the Rice:
- Add the Arborio rice to the pot, stirring to coat it with the onion and garlic mixture. Allow the rice to toast for 1-2 minutes until it becomes slightly translucent around the edges.

Deglaze with Wine:
- Pour in the dry white wine and stir continuously until the wine is mostly absorbed by the rice.

Start Adding the Pumpkin Ale Mixture:

- Begin adding the warm pumpkin ale mixture one ladle at a time, stirring frequently. Allow each addition to be absorbed before adding the next.

Continue Cooking:
- Continue the process of adding liquid and stirring until the rice is creamy and cooked to al dente, which should take about 18-20 minutes.

Finish the Risotto:
- Stir in the grated Parmesan cheese, remaining tablespoon of butter, ground nutmeg, salt, and black pepper. Adjust seasoning to taste.

Garnish and Serve:
- Sprinkle with chopped fresh parsley for garnish and serve the Pumpkin Ale Risotto immediately.

Enjoy this creamy and flavorful Pumpkin Ale Risotto as a comforting fall dish. It pairs well with roasted vegetables, grilled chicken, or as a standalone vegetarian delight.

Beer-Braised Pork Belly

Ingredients:

- 2 lbs pork belly, skin-on, cut into 2-inch cubes
- Salt and black pepper, to taste
- 2 tablespoons vegetable oil
- 1 onion, finely chopped
- 3 cloves garlic, minced
- 2 carrots, peeled and chopped
- 2 celery stalks, chopped
- 1 bottle of your favorite beer (stout or porter works well)
- 2 cups beef or vegetable broth
- 2 tablespoons tomato paste
- 2 bay leaves
- 1 tablespoon brown sugar
- Fresh parsley, chopped (for garnish)

Instructions:

Preheat the Oven:

Preheat your oven to 325°F (163°C).
Prepare the Pork Belly:
- Pat the pork belly cubes dry with paper towels.
- Season the pork belly with salt and black pepper on all sides.

Brown the Pork Belly:
- Heat the vegetable oil in a large, oven-safe Dutch oven over medium-high heat.
- Brown the pork belly cubes on all sides until they develop a golden crust. Work in batches if needed.

Saute Vegetables:
- Add the chopped onion, garlic, carrots, and celery to the Dutch oven. Saute until the vegetables are softened.

Deglaze with Beer:
- Pour in the beer, scraping the bottom of the pot to release any flavorful bits stuck to the surface.

Add Braising Ingredients:

- Stir in the beef or vegetable broth, tomato paste, bay leaves, and brown sugar.

Braise the Pork Belly:
- Return the browned pork belly cubes to the Dutch oven, making sure they are partially submerged in the liquid.
- Cover the Dutch oven with a lid and transfer it to the preheated oven.

Bake:
- Braise the pork belly in the oven for about 2 to 2.5 hours or until the meat is tender and easily pierced with a fork.

Serve:
- Carefully remove the Dutch oven from the oven.
- Discard the bay leaves.
- Serve the beer-braised pork belly over mashed potatoes, polenta, or your favorite side dish.
- Garnish with chopped fresh parsley for a burst of color and freshness.

This Beer-Braised Pork Belly recipe results in tender, flavorful pork belly with a rich and hearty beer-infused sauce. It's a comforting dish that's perfect for special occasions or when you're looking to enjoy a savory, satisfying meal.

Honey Ale Glazed Salmon

Ingredients:

- 4 salmon fillets, skin-on
- Salt and black pepper, to taste
- 1/4 cup honey
- 1/4 cup soy sauce
- 1/4 cup your favorite ale (pale ale or honey ale works well)
- 2 cloves garlic, minced
- 1 tablespoon Dijon mustard
- 1 tablespoon olive oil
- 1 tablespoon fresh ginger, grated
- Sesame seeds and chopped green onions for garnish (optional)

Instructions:

Preheat the Oven:

    Preheat your oven to 400°F (200°C).
    Season the Salmon:
- Pat the salmon fillets dry with paper towels.
- Season both sides of each fillet with salt and black pepper.

    Make the Glaze:
- In a small saucepan, combine honey, soy sauce, ale, minced garlic, Dijon mustard, olive oil, and grated ginger.
- Bring the mixture to a simmer over medium heat and let it simmer for 5-7 minutes or until it thickens slightly. Stir occasionally.

    Glaze the Salmon:
- Place the salmon fillets on a baking sheet lined with parchment paper.
- Brush the glaze over the top of each salmon fillet, ensuring they are well-coated.

    Bake the Salmon:
- Bake in the preheated oven for 12-15 minutes or until the salmon is cooked through and flakes easily with a fork.

    Broil (Optional):

- If you like a caramelized finish, you can broil the salmon for an additional 2-3 minutes under the broiler until the top is golden and caramelized. Keep a close eye to prevent burning.

Garnish and Serve:
- Once cooked, remove the salmon from the oven.
- Garnish with sesame seeds and chopped green onions, if desired.

Serve:
- Serve the Honey Ale Glazed Salmon hot over a bed of rice, quinoa, or your favorite side dishes.

This Honey Ale Glazed Salmon is a perfect balance of sweet and savory, making it a delightful dish for any occasion. The ale-infused glaze adds depth of flavor, creating a memorable meal that's quick and easy to prepare.

Guinness Chocolate Cake

Ingredients:

For the Cake:

- 1 cup Guinness stout
- 1 cup unsalted butter, diced
- 3/4 cup unsweetened cocoa powder
- 2 cups granulated sugar
- 3/4 cup sour cream
- 2 large eggs
- 1 tablespoon vanilla extract
- 2 cups all-purpose flour
- 2 1/2 teaspoons baking soda

For the Cream Cheese Frosting:

- 8 oz cream cheese, softened
- 1 1/2 cups confectioners' sugar
- 1/2 cup heavy cream
- 1 teaspoon vanilla extract

Instructions:

Preheat the Oven:

Preheat your oven to 350°F (175°C). Grease and flour a 9-inch round cake pan or line it with parchment paper.

Prepare the Cake Batter:
- In a saucepan, heat the Guinness and butter over medium heat until the butter is melted.
- Whisk in the cocoa powder and sugar until well combined.
- In a separate bowl, mix together the sour cream, eggs, and vanilla extract.
- Add the sour cream mixture to the Guinness mixture and whisk until smooth.
- Sift in the flour and baking soda, and gently fold until just combined.

Bake the Cake:
- Pour the batter into the prepared cake pan.

- Bake in the preheated oven for 45-50 minutes or until a toothpick inserted into the center comes out clean.
- Allow the cake to cool in the pan for 10 minutes, then transfer it to a wire rack to cool completely.

Prepare the Cream Cheese Frosting:
- In a bowl, beat the softened cream cheese until smooth.
- Add the confectioners' sugar, heavy cream, and vanilla extract. Beat until the frosting is smooth and creamy.

Frost the Cake:
- Once the cake is completely cooled, spread the cream cheese frosting over the top.
- Optionally, decorate with chocolate shavings or a dusting of cocoa powder.

Serve:
- Slice and serve the Guinness Chocolate Cake, savoring the rich and moist texture along with the decadent cream cheese frosting.

This cake is a perfect treat for St. Patrick's Day or any occasion where you want to enjoy the delightful combination of chocolate and Guinness.

Beer and Mustard Glazed Ham

Ingredients:

- 1 fully cooked ham (bone-in or boneless), about 8-10 lbs
- 1 cup brown sugar, packed
- 1/2 cup Dijon mustard
- 1/4 cup whole-grain mustard
- 1/2 cup beer (choose a flavorful beer like a pale ale or lager)
- 2 tablespoons honey
- 1 teaspoon ground cloves (optional)
- 1 teaspoon ground black pepper

Instructions:

Preheat the Oven:

Preheat your oven to 325°F (163°C).

Prepare the Glaze:

In a saucepan over medium heat, combine brown sugar, Dijon mustard, whole-grain mustard, beer, honey, ground cloves (if using), and black pepper. Stir well and simmer for 5-7 minutes, allowing the mixture to thicken slightly.

Score the Ham:

If your ham comes with skin, remove the skin, leaving a thin layer of fat. Score the fat in a diamond pattern using a sharp knife.

Glaze the Ham:
- Place the ham in a roasting pan.
- Brush a generous amount of the beer and mustard glaze over the ham, ensuring it gets into the scored cuts for maximum flavor.

Bake the Ham:
- Bake the ham in the preheated oven, uncovered, for about 1.5 to 2 hours, or until the internal temperature reaches 140°F (60°C), basting with the glaze every 20-30 minutes.

Rest and Carve:

- Once cooked, remove the ham from the oven and let it rest for 15-20 minutes before carving.

Serve:
- Slice the Beer and Mustard Glazed Ham and serve with additional glaze on the side.
- Optionally, garnish with fresh herbs like parsley for a burst of color and freshness.

Enjoy:
- Enjoy the savory and sweet flavors of the Beer and Mustard Glazed Ham as a centerpiece for a festive meal.

This glazed ham is perfect for special occasions, holidays, or any time you want to enjoy a delicious and flavorful main dish.

IPA Pickled Vegetables

Ingredients:

- 2 cups mixed vegetables (carrots, cucumbers, bell peppers, cauliflower, etc.), sliced or cut into bite-sized pieces
- 1 cup IPA (India Pale Ale)
- 1 cup white vinegar
- 1 cup water
- 2 tablespoons sugar
- 1 tablespoon salt
- 1 teaspoon mustard seeds
- 1 teaspoon coriander seeds
- 1 teaspoon black peppercorns
- 2 cloves garlic, minced
- 1 bay leaf
- Optional: red chili flakes for heat

Instructions:

Prepare the Vegetables:
- Clean and cut the vegetables into slices or bite-sized pieces.

Make the Pickling Liquid:
- In a saucepan, combine IPA, white vinegar, water, sugar, salt, mustard seeds, coriander seeds, black peppercorns, minced garlic, and the bay leaf.
- If you like a bit of heat, add red chili flakes to the liquid.

Bring to a Boil:
- Bring the pickling liquid to a boil over medium heat, stirring to dissolve the sugar and salt.

Cool the Liquid:
- Allow the pickling liquid to cool to room temperature.

Pack the Jars:
- Pack the prepared vegetables into clean, sterilized jars.

Pour the Liquid:
- Pour the cooled pickling liquid over the vegetables, ensuring they are fully submerged.

Seal the Jars:

- Seal the jars tightly and refrigerate.

Let it Pickle:
- Allow the IPA pickled vegetables to pickle in the refrigerator for at least 24 hours before consuming.

Serve:
- Serve the IPA pickled vegetables as a tangy and crunchy side dish, or use them as a flavorful addition to salads, sandwiches, or charcuterie boards.

Feel free to experiment with the vegetable combinations and adjust the level of hoppy bitterness by choosing different IPAs. These pickled vegetables are a delightful and unique addition to your culinary repertoire.

Beer and Sriracha Shrimp Skewers

Ingredients:

- 1 pound large shrimp, peeled and deveined
- 1/2 cup your favorite beer (pale ale or lager works well)
- 3 tablespoons Sriracha sauce
- 2 tablespoons soy sauce
- 2 tablespoons honey
- 2 cloves garlic, minced
- 1 tablespoon ginger, grated
- 1 tablespoon olive oil
- Wooden or metal skewers, soaked in water if using wooden ones
- Fresh cilantro, chopped (for garnish)
- Lime wedges (for serving)

Instructions:

Prepare the Marinade:
- In a bowl, whisk together the beer, Sriracha sauce, soy sauce, honey, minced garlic, grated ginger, and olive oil.

Marinate the Shrimp:
- Place the peeled and deveined shrimp in a shallow dish or a resealable plastic bag.
- Pour half of the marinade over the shrimp, reserving the other half for basting and serving.
- Marinate the shrimp in the refrigerator for at least 30 minutes, allowing them to absorb the flavors.

Skewer the Shrimp:
- Preheat your grill or grill pan over medium-high heat.
- Thread the marinated shrimp onto the skewers, distributing them evenly.

Grill the Shrimp:
- Grill the shrimp skewers for 2-3 minutes per side or until they are opaque and cooked through.
- During grilling, baste the shrimp with the reserved marinade for extra flavor.

Garnish and Serve:

- Remove the shrimp skewers from the grill and transfer them to a serving plate.
- Garnish with chopped fresh cilantro and serve with lime wedges on the side.

Serve Hot:
- Serve the Beer and Sriracha Shrimp Skewers hot as an appetizer or main course.

These shrimp skewers are perfect for a barbecue, party, or any occasion where you want to enjoy a spicy and flavorful dish. The combination of beer and Sriracha creates a mouthwatering experience that's sure to be a hit with seafood lovers.

Saison Poached Pears

Ingredients:

- 4 ripe but firm pears, peeled and halved
- 2 cups Saison beer
- 1 cup water
- 1 cup granulated sugar
- 1 cinnamon stick
- 2 whole cloves
- 1 orange, zest peeled into strips
- 1 vanilla bean, split lengthwise
- Whipped cream or vanilla ice cream (for serving, optional)

Instructions:

Prepare the Pears:
- Peel the pears, cut them in half, and remove the cores. Keep the stems intact for a decorative touch.

Prepare the Poaching Liquid:
- In a large saucepan, combine the Saison beer, water, granulated sugar, cinnamon stick, whole cloves, orange zest strips, and the split vanilla bean.

Poach the Pears:
- Place the pear halves into the poaching liquid, ensuring they are submerged.
- Bring the liquid to a simmer over medium heat.

Simmer and Poach:
- Reduce the heat to low, cover the saucepan, and let the pears simmer for about 20-25 minutes or until they are tender but still hold their shape.

Remove from Heat:
- Once the pears are poached, remove the saucepan from the heat and let the pears cool in the liquid.

Serve:
- Once cooled, carefully remove the pears from the poaching liquid.
- Serve the Saison-poached pears on a plate or in a bowl.
- Optionally, drizzle some of the poaching liquid over the pears for extra flavor.

Optional: Reduction of Poaching Liquid:
- If you desire a thicker sauce, you can bring the poaching liquid to a boil and let it reduce to your desired consistency. Remove the cinnamon stick, cloves, and vanilla bean before reducing.

Serve with Whipped Cream or Ice Cream:
- Serve the Saison-poached pears with a dollop of whipped cream or a scoop of vanilla ice cream, if desired.

This dessert is an elegant and flavorful way to showcase the unique characteristics of Saison beer while transforming ordinary pears into a delightful treat. Enjoy the combination of beer-infused sweetness and warm spices in every bite.

Beer and Garlic Roasted Potatoes

Ingredients:

- 2 pounds baby potatoes, washed and halved
- 1/4 cup olive oil
- 1/2 cup your favorite beer (pale ale or lager works well)
- 4 cloves garlic, minced
- 1 teaspoon dried thyme
- 1 teaspoon dried rosemary
- Salt and black pepper, to taste
- Fresh parsley, chopped (for garnish)

Instructions:

Preheat the Oven:

    Preheat your oven to 400°F (200°C).
    Prepare the Potatoes:
- Wash the baby potatoes thoroughly and cut them in half. Pat them dry with a paper towel.

Make the Beer and Garlic Mixture:
- In a bowl, whisk together the olive oil, beer, minced garlic, dried thyme, dried rosemary, salt, and black pepper.

Coat the Potatoes:
- Place the halved potatoes in a large mixing bowl.
- Pour the beer and garlic mixture over the potatoes, ensuring they are well-coated.

Roast the Potatoes:
- Transfer the coated potatoes to a baking sheet, spreading them out in a single layer.
- Roast in the preheated oven for 30-35 minutes or until the potatoes are golden brown and crispy on the edges. Toss the potatoes halfway through the roasting time for even cooking.

Garnish and Serve:
- Once roasted, remove the potatoes from the oven.
- Garnish with chopped fresh parsley for a burst of color and added freshness.

Serve Hot:
- Serve the Beer and Garlic Roasted Potatoes hot as a side dish to complement your main course.

These roasted potatoes are infused with the rich flavors of beer and garlic, creating a delicious and aromatic side dish. Enjoy the crispy exterior and fluffy interior of these potatoes, making them a perfect accompaniment to a variety of meals.

Lager-Battered Shrimp Po' Boy

Ingredients:

For the Lager-Battered Shrimp:

- 1 pound large shrimp, peeled and deveined
- 1 cup all-purpose flour
- 1 teaspoon baking powder
- 1/2 teaspoon salt
- 1/4 teaspoon black pepper
- 1 cup lager beer (choose your favorite)
- Vegetable oil for frying

For the Sandwich:

- Baguette or French bread, cut into sandwich-sized portions
- Shredded lettuce
- Sliced tomatoes
- Sliced dill pickles

For the Remoulade Sauce:

- 1/2 cup mayonnaise
- 2 tablespoons Dijon mustard
- 2 tablespoons sweet pickle relish
- 1 tablespoon hot sauce (adjust to taste)
- 1 teaspoon Worcestershire sauce
- 1 teaspoon paprika
- 1 clove garlic, minced
- Salt and black pepper, to taste

Instructions:

    Prepare the Remoulade Sauce:

- In a bowl, whisk together mayonnaise, Dijon mustard, sweet pickle relish, hot sauce, Worcestershire sauce, paprika, minced garlic, salt, and black pepper. Refrigerate until ready to use.

Make the Lager-Battered Shrimp:
- In a bowl, whisk together flour, baking powder, salt, and black pepper.
- Gradually add the lager beer, whisking continuously until you have a smooth batter.
- Heat vegetable oil in a deep fryer or a large, deep pan to 350°F (180°C).
- Dip each shrimp into the batter, allowing excess to drip off, and carefully place them into the hot oil.
- Fry the shrimp for 2-3 minutes or until golden brown and crispy. Remove with a slotted spoon and place on a paper towel-lined plate to absorb excess oil.

Assemble the Po' Boy:
- Slice the baguette or French bread horizontally, creating a pocket for the filling.
- Spread a generous amount of remoulade sauce on both sides of the bread.
- Layer shredded lettuce, sliced tomatoes, and dill pickles on one side of the bread.
- Arrange the Lager-Battered Shrimp on the other side.

Serve:
- Close the sandwich and press gently to compact the ingredients.
- Serve the Lager-Battered Shrimp Po' Boy immediately, and optionally, with extra remoulade sauce on the side.

This Lager-Battered Shrimp Po' Boy is a flavorful and satisfying sandwich that brings together the crispy goodness of beer-battered shrimp with the creamy and tangy remoulade sauce. Enjoy the delicious combination of textures and flavors in each bite!

Beer and Maple Glazed Carrots

Ingredients:

- 1 pound baby carrots, washed and peeled
- 1/2 cup beer (choose a lager, ale, or any beer with a mild flavor)
- 2 tablespoons maple syrup
- 2 tablespoons unsalted butter
- Salt and black pepper, to taste
- Fresh parsley, chopped (for garnish, optional)

Instructions:

Cook the Carrots:
- In a medium saucepan, bring water to a boil.
- Add the baby carrots and cook for about 5-7 minutes or until they are just tender. Drain and set aside.

Prepare the Glaze:
- In a large skillet, combine the beer, maple syrup, and unsalted butter over medium heat.
- Bring the mixture to a simmer, stirring to combine the ingredients.

Add Carrots to the Glaze:
- Add the cooked baby carrots to the skillet, tossing them in the glaze to coat evenly.

Simmer and Glaze:
- Allow the carrots to simmer in the glaze for 5-7 minutes, or until the glaze has thickened slightly and coats the carrots.

Season:
- Season the glazed carrots with salt and black pepper, adjusting to taste.

Garnish and Serve:
- Transfer the glazed carrots to a serving dish.
- Garnish with chopped fresh parsley, if desired.

Serve Hot:
- Serve the Beer and Maple Glazed Carrots hot as a side dish alongside your main course.

These glazed carrots are a perfect combination of sweetness from the maple syrup and depth of flavor from the beer. The glaze adds a delicious coating to the tender carrots, making them a delightful addition to your meal. Enjoy the rich and comforting taste of beer and maple in this easy-to-make side dish!

Double IPA Barbecue Sauce

Ingredients:

- 1 cup Double IPA beer
- 1 cup ketchup
- 1/2 cup apple cider vinegar
- 1/3 cup brown sugar
- 1/4 cup molasses
- 2 tablespoons Dijon mustard
- 1 tablespoon Worcestershire sauce
- 1 teaspoon onion powder
- 1 teaspoon garlic powder
- 1/2 teaspoon smoked paprika
- 1/2 teaspoon black pepper
- 1/2 teaspoon salt
- 1/4 teaspoon cayenne pepper (adjust to taste)

Instructions:

Combine Ingredients:
- In a saucepan over medium heat, combine Double IPA beer, ketchup, apple cider vinegar, brown sugar, molasses, Dijon mustard, Worcestershire sauce, onion powder, garlic powder, smoked paprika, black pepper, salt, and cayenne pepper.

Bring to a Simmer:
- Whisk the ingredients together and bring the mixture to a simmer.

Simmer and Thicken:
- Let the sauce simmer for 15-20 minutes, stirring occasionally. This allows the flavors to meld and the sauce to thicken.

Adjust Seasonings:
- Taste the barbecue sauce and adjust the seasonings according to your preference. Add more cayenne for heat or more brown sugar for sweetness.

Cool and Store:
- Allow the Double IPA barbecue sauce to cool to room temperature.
- Transfer it to a jar or airtight container for storage.

Use as a Glaze or Dip:

- Use the Double IPA barbecue sauce as a glaze for grilled meats or as a dipping sauce. Brush it on during the last few minutes of grilling for a flavorful finish.

This Double IPA barbecue sauce brings a bold and hoppy flavor to your barbecue dishes. The combination of the beer's hoppiness with the sweetness and smokiness of the other ingredients creates a unique and delicious sauce. Enjoy it on grilled chicken, ribs, burgers, or any barbecue favorites!

Beer-Braised Beef Stew

Ingredients:

- 2 pounds beef stew meat, cut into bite-sized pieces
- Salt and black pepper, to taste
- 1/2 cup all-purpose flour, for dredging
- 2-3 tablespoons vegetable oil
- 1 large onion, chopped
- 3 cloves garlic, minced
- 2 carrots, peeled and sliced
- 2 celery stalks, sliced
- 1 bottle of your favorite beer (stout or ale works well)
- 2 cups beef broth
- 2 tablespoons tomato paste
- 1 tablespoon Worcestershire sauce
- 2 bay leaves
- 1 teaspoon dried thyme
- 1 teaspoon smoked paprika
- 1 pound baby potatoes, halved
- Chopped fresh parsley, for garnish (optional)

Instructions:

Preheat the Oven:

> Preheat your oven to 325°F (163°C).
> Season and Dredge the Beef:
> - Season the beef stew meat with salt and black pepper.
> - Dredge the meat in flour, shaking off excess.
>
> Brown the Beef:
> - In a large oven-safe pot or Dutch oven, heat vegetable oil over medium-high heat.
> - Brown the beef in batches until well-seared on all sides. Remove and set aside.
>
> Saute Vegetables:
> - In the same pot, add chopped onion, minced garlic, sliced carrots, and sliced celery. Saute until the vegetables are softened.
>
> Deglaze with Beer:

- Pour in the beer, scraping the bottom of the pot to release any flavorful bits.

Add Braising Ingredients:
- Return the browned beef to the pot.
- Add beef broth, tomato paste, Worcestershire sauce, bay leaves, dried thyme, and smoked paprika. Stir to combine.

Braise in the Oven:
- Cover the pot and transfer it to the preheated oven.
- Braise for 2 to 2.5 hours or until the beef is tender.

Add Potatoes:
- About 30 minutes before the stew is done, add the halved baby potatoes to the pot. Stir to combine.

Check and Adjust:
- Check the seasoning and adjust with salt and pepper if needed.

Serve:
- Remove the bay leaves.
- Serve the beer-braised beef stew hot, garnished with chopped fresh parsley if desired.

This beer-braised beef stew is a comforting and hearty dish, perfect for warming up on chilly days. The beer adds depth and richness to the stew, making it a flavorful and satisfying meal. Enjoy it with crusty bread or over mashed potatoes for a complete dining experience.

Pumpkin Ale Cheesecake

Ingredients:

For the Crust:

- 1 1/2 cups graham cracker crumbs
- 1/4 cup melted butter
- 1/4 cup granulated sugar

For the Cheesecake Filling:

- 3 packages (24 ounces) cream cheese, softened
- 1 cup granulated sugar
- 3 large eggs
- 1 cup canned pumpkin puree
- 1/2 cup pumpkin ale
- 1 teaspoon vanilla extract
- 1 teaspoon ground cinnamon
- 1/2 teaspoon ground nutmeg
- 1/4 teaspoon ground cloves
- 1/4 teaspoon salt

For the Topping:

- Whipped cream
- Caramel sauce
- Crushed graham crackers

Instructions:

Preheat the Oven:

    Preheat your oven to 325°F (163°C).
    Prepare the Crust:
- In a bowl, combine graham cracker crumbs, melted butter, and granulated sugar.

- Press the mixture into the bottom of a 9-inch springform pan to form the crust.

Bake the Crust:
- Bake the crust in the preheated oven for 10 minutes. Remove and let it cool while you prepare the filling.

Prepare the Cheesecake Filling:
- In a large mixing bowl, beat the cream cheese until smooth.
- Add the sugar and beat until well combined.
- Add the eggs, one at a time, beating well after each addition.
- Add the pumpkin puree, pumpkin ale, vanilla extract, ground cinnamon, ground nutmeg, ground cloves, and salt. Mix until smooth and well combined.

Pour the Filling:
- Pour the cheesecake filling over the baked crust in the springform pan.

Bake the Cheesecake:
- Bake in the preheated oven for 60-70 minutes or until the center is set and the top is lightly browned.
- Turn off the oven and let the cheesecake cool in the oven with the door ajar for about 1 hour.

Chill the Cheesecake:
- Remove the cheesecake from the oven and refrigerate for at least 4 hours or overnight.

Top and Serve:
- Before serving, spread whipped cream over the top, drizzle with caramel sauce, and sprinkle crushed graham crackers for added texture.

Slice and Enjoy:
- Slice the Pumpkin Ale Cheesecake and serve chilled.

This Pumpkin Ale Cheesecake is a delightful and festive dessert, perfect for autumn gatherings or Thanksgiving celebrations. The addition of pumpkin ale adds a unique twist to the classic cheesecake, creating a rich and flavorful treat.

Stout and Coffee BBQ Ribs

Ingredients:

For the Ribs:

- 2 racks of baby back ribs
- Salt and black pepper, to taste

For the Stout and Coffee BBQ Sauce:

- 1 cup stout beer
- 1/2 cup strong brewed coffee (cooled)
- 1 cup ketchup
- 1/4 cup apple cider vinegar
- 1/4 cup brown sugar
- 2 tablespoons Dijon mustard
- 2 tablespoons Worcestershire sauce
- 2 cloves garlic, minced
- 1 teaspoon smoked paprika
- 1 teaspoon onion powder
- 1/2 teaspoon black pepper
- 1/2 teaspoon salt
- 1/4 teaspoon cayenne pepper (optional for heat)

Instructions:

Preheat the Oven:

> Preheat your oven to 300°F (150°C).
> Prepare the Ribs:
> - Remove the membrane from the back of the ribs.
> - Season the ribs with salt and black pepper.
>
> Slow Cook the Ribs:
> - Place the seasoned ribs on a baking sheet lined with aluminum foil.
> - Cover the ribs tightly with another layer of foil.

- Bake in the preheated oven for 2.5 to 3 hours or until the ribs are tender and cooked through.

Prepare the BBQ Sauce:
- In a saucepan, combine stout beer, brewed coffee, ketchup, apple cider vinegar, brown sugar, Dijon mustard, Worcestershire sauce, minced garlic, smoked paprika, onion powder, black pepper, salt, and cayenne pepper (if using).
- Bring the mixture to a simmer over medium heat. Let it simmer for about 15-20 minutes, stirring occasionally, until the sauce thickens.

Grill the Ribs:
- Preheat your grill to medium-high heat.
- Remove the ribs from the oven and carefully transfer them to the preheated grill.

Apply BBQ Sauce:
- Brush the ribs generously with the Stout and Coffee BBQ sauce.
- Grill the ribs for 10-15 minutes, turning and basting with more sauce, until they have a nice caramelized crust.

Rest and Slice:
- Remove the ribs from the grill and let them rest for a few minutes.
- Slice the ribs between the bones.

Serve:
- Serve the Stout and Coffee BBQ Ribs hot, with extra sauce on the side for dipping.

These ribs are a perfect blend of smoky, sweet, and rich flavors. The combination of stout beer and coffee in the barbecue sauce adds depth and complexity, making these ribs a standout dish for any barbecue or gathering. Enjoy the bold and delicious taste!

Beer and Cheddar Bread

Ingredients:

- 3 cups all-purpose flour
- 1 tablespoon sugar
- 1 tablespoon baking powder
- 1 teaspoon salt
- 1 1/2 cups sharp cheddar cheese, shredded
- 12 oz beer (choose a beer with a robust flavor)
- 1/4 cup unsalted butter, melted
- 1 tablespoon fresh parsley, chopped (optional, for garnish)

Instructions:

Preheat the Oven:

Preheat your oven to 375°F (190°C). Grease a standard-sized loaf pan.

Mix Dry Ingredients:

In a large mixing bowl, whisk together the flour, sugar, baking powder, and salt.

Add Cheddar Cheese:

Stir in the shredded cheddar cheese until it's evenly distributed throughout the dry ingredients.

Pour in Beer:

Pour in the beer and stir until just combined. The batter will be thick and sticky.

Transfer to Pan:

Transfer the batter into the greased loaf pan, spreading it out evenly.

Pour Melted Butter:

Pour the melted butter evenly over the top of the batter.

Bake:

Bake in the preheated oven for 45-55 minutes or until the top is golden brown and a toothpick inserted into the center comes out clean.

Cool and Garnish:
- Allow the Beer and Cheddar Bread to cool in the pan for about 10 minutes.
- Optional: Sprinkle chopped fresh parsley on top for garnish.

Slice and Serve:
- Transfer the bread to a wire rack to cool completely before slicing.
- Slice and serve the Beer and Cheddar Bread on its own or as a side to soups and stews.

This Beer and Cheddar Bread is perfect for beer lovers and cheese enthusiasts alike. The beer adds depth of flavor and a moist texture to the bread, while the cheddar cheese provides a delightful savory kick. Enjoy it fresh out of the oven or toasted with your favorite spreads!

Ale-Braised Sausages with Peppers and Onions

Ingredients:

- 1 to 1.5 pounds of your favorite sausages (such as Italian, bratwurst, or kielbasa)
- 2 tablespoons olive oil
- 1 large onion, thinly sliced
- 2 bell peppers (different colors), thinly sliced
- 3 cloves garlic, minced
- 1 cup ale or beer (choose a flavorful ale)
- 1 cup chicken or vegetable broth
- 1 tablespoon tomato paste
- 1 teaspoon dried oregano
- 1 teaspoon dried thyme
- 1 bay leaf
- Salt and black pepper, to taste
- Fresh parsley, chopped (for garnish)
- Crusty bread or rolls (for serving)

Instructions:

Brown the Sausages:
- In a large skillet or Dutch oven, heat olive oil over medium-high heat.
- Brown the sausages on all sides until they develop a nice crust. Remove them from the skillet and set aside.

Saute Peppers, Onions, and Garlic:
- In the same skillet, add sliced onions and bell peppers. Sauté until they start to soften, about 5 minutes.
- Add minced garlic and sauté for an additional 1-2 minutes until fragrant.

Deglaze with Ale:
- Pour in the ale or beer, scraping the bottom of the skillet to release any flavorful bits.

Add Braising Ingredients:
- Stir in chicken or vegetable broth, tomato paste, dried oregano, dried thyme, bay leaf, salt, and black pepper.

Braise the Sausages:
- Return the browned sausages to the skillet, nestling them into the peppers and onions.

- Bring the liquid to a simmer, then reduce the heat to low, cover, and let it simmer for 20-25 minutes until the sausages are fully cooked and the flavors meld.

Adjust Seasonings:
- Taste the braising liquid and adjust the seasoning if necessary.

Serve:
- Discard the bay leaf.
- Serve the Ale-Braised Sausages with Peppers and Onions over crusty bread or rolls.
- Garnish with chopped fresh parsley.

Enjoy:
- Enjoy this comforting and flavorful dish with a side of your favorite accompaniments.

This Ale-Braised Sausages with Peppers and Onions recipe is perfect for a cozy and satisfying meal. The ale-infused braising liquid adds depth to the sausages, while the peppers and onions contribute a sweet and savory combination. Serve it as a standalone dish or with a side of mashed potatoes, rice, or pasta.

Beer and Rosemary Focaccia

Ingredients:

For the Focaccia:

- 3 1/2 cups all-purpose flour
- 1 1/4 cups warm beer (at about 110°F or 43°C)
- 2 teaspoons sugar
- 1 packet (2 1/4 teaspoons) active dry yeast
- 1 teaspoon salt
- 1/4 cup olive oil (plus extra for greasing and drizzling)

For the Topping:

- Fresh rosemary leaves, chopped
- Coarse sea salt

Instructions:

Activate the Yeast:
- In a bowl, combine warm beer and sugar. Stir until the sugar dissolves.
- Sprinkle the active dry yeast over the beer mixture. Let it sit for about 5-10 minutes, or until it becomes frothy.

Prepare the Dough:
- In a large mixing bowl, combine the activated yeast mixture with the flour and salt.
- Gradually add the olive oil while stirring, and continue to mix until a dough forms.

Knead the Dough:
- Turn the dough onto a floured surface and knead for about 5-7 minutes, or until it becomes smooth and elastic.

First Rise:
- Place the dough in a lightly oiled bowl, cover it with a clean kitchen towel, and let it rise in a warm place for 1-1.5 hours, or until it doubles in size.

Preheat the Oven:
- Preheat your oven to 425°F (220°C).

Shape the Focaccia:
- Punch down the risen dough and transfer it to a greased baking sheet.
- Spread and press the dough onto the baking sheet, creating a rectangle or oval shape.

Second Rise:
- Cover the dough with a clean kitchen towel and let it rise for another 20-30 minutes.

Make Indentations:
- Use your fingertips to make deep indentations all over the dough.

Drizzle with Olive Oil and Add Toppings:
- Drizzle the dough generously with olive oil.
- Sprinkle chopped fresh rosemary leaves and coarse sea salt over the top.

Bake:
- Bake in the preheated oven for 20-25 minutes or until the focaccia is golden brown and sounds hollow when tapped.

Cool and Serve:
- Allow the Beer and Rosemary Focaccia to cool slightly before slicing.
- Serve warm and enjoy!

This Beer and Rosemary Focaccia is a wonderful accompaniment to soups, salads, or enjoyed on its own. The beer adds depth to the flavor of the bread, and the rosemary provides a fragrant and herby touch. It's perfect for sharing with friends and family.

Honey Ale Glazed Brussels Sprouts

Ingredients:

- 1 pound Brussels sprouts, trimmed and halved
- 2 tablespoons olive oil
- Salt and black pepper, to taste
- 1/2 cup honey
- 1/4 cup ale or beer (choose a mild ale)
- 2 tablespoons whole grain mustard
- 2 tablespoons balsamic vinegar
- Crushed red pepper flakes, to taste (optional, for heat)
- Chopped fresh parsley, for garnish (optional)

Instructions:

Preheat the Oven:

Preheat your oven to 400°F (200°C).
Prepare the Brussels Sprouts:
- In a large mixing bowl, toss the halved Brussels sprouts with olive oil, salt, and black pepper until evenly coated.

Roast Brussels Sprouts:
- Spread the Brussels sprouts in a single layer on a baking sheet.
- Roast in the preheated oven for 20-25 minutes or until the sprouts are golden brown and crispy on the edges. Toss them halfway through roasting for even cooking.

Prepare the Glaze:
- While the Brussels sprouts are roasting, make the honey ale glaze.
- In a saucepan over medium heat, combine honey, ale, whole grain mustard, balsamic vinegar, and optional crushed red pepper flakes.
- Bring the mixture to a simmer, stirring frequently. Let it simmer for 5-7 minutes or until the glaze thickens slightly.

Glaze the Brussels Sprouts:
- Once the Brussels sprouts are roasted, transfer them to a large bowl.
- Pour the honey ale glaze over the roasted Brussels sprouts and toss to coat them evenly.

Garnish and Serve:

- Garnish with chopped fresh parsley, if desired.
- Serve the Honey Ale Glazed Brussels Sprouts hot as a side dish.

These Honey Ale Glazed Brussels Sprouts are a delightful balance of sweetness and savory flavors. The ale adds a depth of flavor to the honey glaze, creating a delicious coating for the roasted Brussels sprouts. This dish is perfect for holiday dinners or as a flavorful side for any occasion.

Beer and Dijon Mustard Chicken Thighs

Ingredients:

- 4-6 bone-in, skin-on chicken thighs
- Salt and black pepper, to taste
- 1 tablespoon olive oil
- 1 onion, finely chopped
- 3 cloves garlic, minced
- 1 cup beer (choose a lager or ale)
- 3 tablespoons Dijon mustard
- 2 tablespoons honey
- 1 tablespoon whole grain mustard
- 1 teaspoon dried thyme
- Fresh parsley, chopped (for garnish, optional)

Instructions:

Preheat the Oven:

Preheat your oven to 375°F (190°C).
Season the Chicken Thighs:
- Season the chicken thighs with salt and black pepper on both sides.

Sear the Chicken:
- In an oven-safe skillet, heat olive oil over medium-high heat.
- Sear the chicken thighs, skin side down, until golden brown. Flip and sear the other side. Remove the chicken from the skillet and set aside.

Saute Onion and Garlic:
- In the same skillet, add chopped onion and sauté until softened.
- Add minced garlic and sauté for an additional minute until fragrant.

Prepare the Sauce:
- Pour in the beer to deglaze the skillet, scraping up any browned bits.
- Stir in Dijon mustard, honey, whole grain mustard, and dried thyme. Mix until well combined.

Simmer and Return Chicken:
- Let the sauce simmer for a few minutes until it thickens slightly.
- Return the seared chicken thighs to the skillet, coating them with the sauce.

Bake in the Oven:
- Transfer the skillet to the preheated oven.
- Bake for 25-30 minutes or until the chicken thighs are cooked through, and the skin is crispy.

Garnish and Serve:
- Garnish with chopped fresh parsley if desired.
- Serve the Beer and Dijon Mustard Chicken Thighs hot, with the sauce spooned over the top.

These Beer and Dijon Mustard Chicken Thighs are succulent, flavorful, and have a deliciously crispy skin. The combination of beer and Dijon mustard creates a mouthwatering sauce that complements the chicken perfectly. Serve this dish with your favorite side dishes for a complete and satisfying meal.

IPA Citrus Sorbet

Ingredients:

- 1 cup water
- 1 cup granulated sugar
- 1 cup IPA beer (choose a citrus-forward IPA)
- Zest of 2 citrus fruits (e.g., oranges, grapefruits, or a combination)
- 1/2 cup fresh citrus juice (from the same fruits used for zest)

Instructions:

Prepare Simple Syrup:
- In a saucepan, combine water and granulated sugar over medium heat.
- Stir until the sugar dissolves completely, creating a simple syrup.
- Allow the syrup to cool to room temperature.

Combine Ingredients:
- In a mixing bowl, combine the cooled simple syrup, IPA beer, citrus zest, and fresh citrus juice.
- Mix well to ensure all ingredients are thoroughly combined.

Chill Mixture:
- Place the mixture in the refrigerator and let it chill for at least 1-2 hours to enhance the flavors.

Freeze in Sorbet Maker:
- Pour the chilled mixture into your ice cream maker.
- Follow the manufacturer's instructions for your specific machine to churn the sorbet until it reaches a slushy, frozen consistency.

Transfer to Freezer Container:
- Transfer the partially frozen sorbet into a lidded freezer-safe container.

Finish Freezing:
- Allow the IPA Citrus Sorbet to freeze completely in the container for at least 4-6 hours or overnight.

Serve:
- When ready to serve, let the sorbet sit at room temperature for a few minutes to soften slightly.
- Scoop the sorbet into bowls or cones.

Garnish (Optional):
- Garnish with additional citrus zest or a slice of citrus on top.

Enjoy:
- Enjoy the refreshing and hoppy flavors of IPA Citrus Sorbet!

This IPA Citrus Sorbet is a unique and delightful frozen treat that combines the bright, citrusy notes of the beer with the refreshing taste of citrus fruits. It's a perfect way to cool down on a warm day or as a palate cleanser between courses. Adjust the sweetness and citrus intensity to suit your taste preferences.

Beer-Battered Avocado Fries

Ingredients:

- 2 large avocados, peeled, pitted, and sliced into wedges
- 1 cup all-purpose flour
- 1 teaspoon baking powder
- 1/2 teaspoon salt
- 1/2 teaspoon black pepper
- 1 cup beer (choose a light and crisp beer)
- Vegetable oil for frying
- Optional: Dipping sauce (such as spicy mayo or chipotle ranch)

Instructions:

Prepare Avocado Wedges:
- Cut the avocados in half, remove the pit, and slice each half into wedges.

Prepare Beer Batter:
- In a mixing bowl, whisk together the flour, baking powder, salt, and black pepper.
- Pour in the beer and whisk until you have a smooth batter. The consistency should be similar to pancake batter.

Heat Oil for Frying:
- In a heavy-bottomed pot or deep fryer, heat vegetable oil to 350°F (175°C).

Coat Avocado Wedges:
- Dip each avocado wedge into the beer batter, ensuring it's fully coated.

Fry the Avocado Fries:
- Carefully place the beer-battered avocado wedges into the hot oil, a few at a time, to avoid overcrowding.
- Fry for 2-3 minutes or until golden brown and crispy. Flip them halfway through for even cooking.

Drain and Repeat:
- Use a slotted spoon or tongs to transfer the fried avocado fries to a plate lined with paper towels to drain excess oil.
- Repeat the process until all avocado wedges are fried.

Serve:
- Serve the Beer-Battered Avocado Fries hot and crispy.
- Optionally, pair them with your favorite dipping sauce.

Enjoy:
- Enjoy the creamy and crispy goodness of Beer-Battered Avocado Fries!

These avocado fries make a fantastic appetizer or snack, and the beer batter adds a delightful twist to the traditional frying method. The creamy avocado contrasts beautifully with the crispy exterior, creating a delicious and satisfying bite. Serve them with a dipping sauce of your choice for an extra burst of flavor.

Beer and Honey Glazed Roasted Nuts

Ingredients:

- 3 cups mixed nuts (such as almonds, walnuts, pecans, and cashews)
- 1/4 cup unsalted butter
- 1/4 cup honey
- 1/4 cup brown sugar
- 1/2 cup beer (choose a malt-forward beer)
- 1 teaspoon ground cinnamon
- 1/2 teaspoon ground nutmeg
- 1/2 teaspoon salt
- Optional: A pinch of cayenne pepper for a hint of heat

Instructions:

Preheat the Oven:

    Preheat your oven to 350°F (175°C).
    Prepare the Nuts:
- Spread the mixed nuts evenly on a baking sheet lined with parchment paper.

Roast the Nuts:
- Roast the nuts in the preheated oven for 10-12 minutes or until they are lightly golden and fragrant. Stir them halfway through for even roasting.

Prepare Glaze:
- In a saucepan over medium heat, melt the butter.
- Add honey, brown sugar, beer, ground cinnamon, ground nutmeg, salt, and cayenne pepper (if using).
- Stir the mixture continuously until it comes to a simmer.

Simmer and Thicken:
- Let the glaze simmer for about 5-7 minutes or until it thickens slightly. Stir occasionally to prevent sticking.

Combine Nuts and Glaze:
- Once the nuts are roasted, transfer them to a large mixing bowl.
- Pour the beer and honey glaze over the roasted nuts and toss until the nuts are well-coated.

Bake Again:
- Spread the glazed nuts back onto the parchment-lined baking sheet.

- Bake for an additional 10-12 minutes, stirring halfway through, until the nuts are caramelized and the glaze is set.

Cool and Break Apart:
- Allow the Beer and Honey Glazed Roasted Nuts to cool completely on the baking sheet.
- Break apart any clusters if needed.

Store:
- Once fully cooled, store the glazed nuts in an airtight container.

Enjoy:
- Enjoy these sweet and savory Beer and Honey Glazed Roasted Nuts as a snack or party treat!

These glazed nuts are perfect for serving at gatherings, parties, or as a delicious snack during a cozy night. The combination of beer and honey adds a unique depth of flavor to the classic roasted nuts, making them a delightful treat for any occasion.

Pale Ale Lemon Bars

Ingredients:

For the Crust:

- 1 cup all-purpose flour
- 1/2 cup unsalted butter, softened
- 1/4 cup powdered sugar

For the Lemon Filling:

- 4 large eggs
- 1 1/2 cups granulated sugar
- 1/3 cup all-purpose flour
- 1/2 cup fresh lemon juice (about 3-4 lemons)
- Zest of 1 lemon
- 1/4 cup pale ale beer
- Powdered sugar for dusting (optional)

Instructions:

Preheat the Oven:

Preheat your oven to 350°F (175°C) and line a 9x9-inch (23x23 cm) baking pan with parchment paper, leaving an overhang on two sides for easy removal.
Prepare the Crust:
- In a bowl, combine the flour, softened butter, and powdered sugar.
- Press the mixture into the bottom of the prepared baking pan to form an even crust.

Bake the Crust:
- Bake the crust in the preheated oven for 15-18 minutes or until lightly golden. Remove from the oven and set aside.

Prepare the Lemon Filling:
- In a mixing bowl, whisk together the eggs and granulated sugar until well combined.

- Add the flour, fresh lemon juice, lemon zest, and pale ale beer. Whisk until smooth.

Pour Filling over the Crust:
- Pour the lemon filling over the pre-baked crust.

Bake the Bars:
- Bake in the oven for 20-25 minutes or until the edges are set, and the center is slightly firm.

Cool and Chill:
- Allow the Pale Ale Lemon Bars to cool completely in the pan.
- Once cooled, refrigerate for at least 2 hours to chill and set.

Slice and Dust:
- Lift the bars out of the pan using the parchment overhang.
- Cut into squares or bars.
- Dust with powdered sugar before serving if desired.

Serve:
- Serve these Pale Ale Lemon Bars chilled and enjoy the delightful combination of citrusy and beer-infused flavors.

These bars offer a refreshing twist with the addition of pale ale, adding complexity to the classic lemony goodness. They are perfect for dessert tables, picnics, or any occasion where you want to impress with a unique and flavorful treat.

Beer and Chipotle Pulled Pork

Ingredients:

- 3-4 pounds pork shoulder or pork butt, trimmed of excess fat
- Salt and black pepper, to taste
- 2 tablespoons vegetable oil
- 1 large onion, finely chopped
- 4 cloves garlic, minced
- 1 can (12 ounces) beer (choose a flavorful beer like a stout or amber ale)
- 1 can (7 ounces) chipotle peppers in adobo sauce, finely chopped
- 1/4 cup brown sugar
- 2 teaspoons ground cumin
- 2 teaspoons dried oregano
- 1 teaspoon smoked paprika
- 1/2 teaspoon ground cinnamon
- 1 cup chicken or beef broth
- Juice of 2 limes

Instructions:

Preheat the Oven:

    Preheat your oven to 325°F (163°C).

Season and Sear the Pork:
- Season the pork shoulder with salt and black pepper.
- In a large oven-safe pot or Dutch oven, heat vegetable oil over medium-high heat.
- Sear the pork on all sides until browned. Remove and set aside.

Saute Onions and Garlic:
- In the same pot, add chopped onions and sauté until softened.
- Add minced garlic and sauté for an additional minute until fragrant.

Add Beer and Chipotle Peppers:
- Pour in the beer to deglaze the pot, scraping up any browned bits.
- Stir in the finely chopped chipotle peppers in adobo sauce.

Combine Spices and Brown Sugar:
- Add brown sugar, ground cumin, dried oregano, smoked paprika, and ground cinnamon. Mix well.

Add Pork and Broth:

- Return the seared pork to the pot.
- Pour in the chicken or beef broth.

Bake in the Oven:
- Cover the pot with a lid and transfer it to the preheated oven.
- Bake for 3-4 hours or until the pork is fork-tender and easily pulls apart.

Shred the Pork:
- Once cooked, use two forks to shred the pork in the pot.

Add Lime Juice:
- Squeeze the juice of two limes over the pulled pork and mix.

Adjust Seasoning:
- Taste and adjust the seasoning, adding more salt, pepper, or lime juice if needed.

Serve:
- Serve the Beer and Chipotle Pulled Pork in tacos, sandwiches, or over rice.

This Beer and Chipotle Pulled Pork is packed with bold and smoky flavors, making it a versatile dish for various meals. Whether you enjoy it in tacos, sandwiches, or served over rice, this pulled pork is sure to be a crowd-pleaser with its deliciously complex taste.

Guinness Beef Chili

Ingredients:

- 2 pounds ground beef
- 1 large onion, finely chopped
- 4 cloves garlic, minced
- 2 bell peppers (any color), diced
- 2 cans (14 ounces each) kidney beans, drained and rinsed
- 1 can (28 ounces) crushed tomatoes
- 1 can (14 ounces) diced tomatoes
- 1 cup Guinness beer
- 2 tablespoons tomato paste
- 3 tablespoons chili powder
- 1 tablespoon ground cumin
- 1 tablespoon smoked paprika
- 1 teaspoon dried oregano
- 1 teaspoon ground coriander
- 1 teaspoon salt (or to taste)
- 1/2 teaspoon black pepper (or to taste)
- 1-2 tablespoons vegetable oil
- Optional toppings: shredded cheddar cheese, sour cream, chopped green onions, and fresh cilantro

Instructions:

Brown the Beef:
- In a large pot or Dutch oven, heat vegetable oil over medium-high heat.
- Add ground beef and cook until browned. Drain excess fat if needed.

Saute Vegetables:
- Add chopped onions, minced garlic, and diced bell peppers to the pot. Saute until vegetables are softened.

Add Spices:
- Stir in chili powder, ground cumin, smoked paprika, dried oregano, ground coriander, salt, and black pepper. Mix well to coat the meat and vegetables with the spices.

Tomatoes and Tomato Paste:
- Add crushed tomatoes, diced tomatoes, and tomato paste to the pot. Stir to combine.

Pour in Guinness:
- Pour in the Guinness beer and mix to incorporate the flavors.

Add Beans:
- Add kidney beans to the pot and stir.

Simmer:
- Bring the chili to a simmer, then reduce the heat to low. Cover the pot and let it simmer for at least 1-2 hours, stirring occasionally. The longer it simmers, the more the flavors will meld.

Adjust Seasoning:
- Taste the chili and adjust the seasoning if needed. Add more salt, pepper, or chili powder according to your preference.

Serve:
- Serve the Guinness Beef Chili hot, garnished with shredded cheddar cheese, sour cream, chopped green onions, and fresh cilantro if desired.

This Guinness Beef Chili is perfect for warming up on a cold day or for a comforting meal. The addition of Guinness beer adds depth and complexity to the chili, creating a rich and satisfying dish. Enjoy it with your favorite toppings and sides for a complete and hearty meal.

Beer and Basil Grilled Corn on the Cob

Ingredients:

- 4 ears of fresh corn, husked
- 1/2 cup unsalted butter, melted
- 1/4 cup fresh basil, finely chopped
- 1/4 cup beer (choose a light and crisp beer)
- Salt and black pepper, to taste
- Optional: Grated Parmesan cheese for serving

Instructions:

Preheat the Grill:
- Preheat your grill to medium-high heat.

Prepare the Basil Butter:
- In a small bowl, combine melted butter, chopped fresh basil, and beer. Mix well.

Grill the Corn:
- Place the husked ears of corn directly on the preheated grill grates.

Baste with Basil Beer Butter:
- Use a basting brush to generously brush the basil beer butter over each ear of corn. Make sure to coat them evenly.

Grill and Rotate:
- Grill the corn for about 10-15 minutes, turning them occasionally to ensure even cooking. Continue to baste with the basil beer butter throughout the grilling process.

Season:
- Sprinkle salt and black pepper over the corn during the last few minutes of grilling, adjusting to taste.

Check for Doneness:
- The corn is done when the kernels are tender and have a nice char from the grill.

Serve:
- Remove the Beer and Basil Grilled Corn on the Cob from the grill.
- Optional: Sprinkle grated Parmesan cheese over the hot corn before serving.

Enjoy:

- Serve the grilled corn hot and enjoy the delicious combination of beer and basil flavors.

This Beer and Basil Grilled Corn on the Cob is a perfect side dish for summer barbecues or outdoor gatherings. The beer adds a subtle depth of flavor, and the basil butter enhances the natural sweetness of the corn. It's a simple yet impressive way to elevate your grilled corn experience.

Beer-Braised Chicken Tacos

Ingredients:

For the Beer-Braised Chicken:

- 1.5 to 2 pounds boneless, skinless chicken thighs
- Salt and black pepper, to taste
- 2 tablespoons vegetable oil
- 1 large onion, finely chopped
- 4 cloves garlic, minced
- 1 teaspoon ground cumin
- 1 teaspoon chili powder
- 1 teaspoon dried oregano
- 1 cup beer (choose a lager or pale ale)
- 1 cup chicken broth
- Juice of 1 lime

For Serving:

- Corn or flour tortillas
- Shredded lettuce
- Diced tomatoes
- Shredded cheese
- Sour cream
- Fresh cilantro, chopped
- Lime wedges

Instructions:

Season and Brown the Chicken:
- Season chicken thighs with salt and black pepper.
- In a large skillet or Dutch oven, heat vegetable oil over medium-high heat.
- Brown the chicken thighs on both sides. Remove and set aside.

Saute Onion and Garlic:
- In the same skillet, add chopped onion and sauté until softened.
- Add minced garlic and sauté for an additional minute.

Spices and Braising Liquid:
- Stir in ground cumin, chili powder, and dried oregano.

- Pour in beer, chicken broth, and lime juice. Mix well.

Braise the Chicken:
- Return the browned chicken thighs to the skillet, nestling them into the liquid.
- Bring the liquid to a simmer, then reduce the heat to low. Cover and let it simmer for 25-30 minutes or until the chicken is tender and cooked through.

Shred the Chicken:
- Once cooked, use two forks to shred the chicken in the skillet. Allow it to absorb the flavorful braising liquid.

Serve:
- Warm the tortillas and fill them with the shredded beer-braised chicken.
- Top with shredded lettuce, diced tomatoes, shredded cheese, sour cream, and chopped cilantro.

Garnish and Enjoy:
- Garnish with lime wedges and additional cilantro.
- Serve the Beer-Braised Chicken Tacos hot and enjoy!

These Beer-Braised Chicken Tacos are packed with savory and aromatic flavors, making them a delicious and satisfying meal. The beer-infused braising liquid adds a unique depth to the shredded chicken, creating a flavorful taco filling. Customize the toppings to suit your preferences and enjoy a tasty taco night.

Brown Ale and Mushroom Risotto

Ingredients:

- 1 1/2 cups Arborio rice
- 1 cup brown ale
- 4 cups chicken or vegetable broth, kept warm
- 1 cup assorted mushrooms, sliced (e.g., cremini, shiitake, oyster)
- 1 small onion, finely chopped
- 2 cloves garlic, minced
- 1/2 cup Parmesan cheese, grated
- 2 tablespoons unsalted butter
- 2 tablespoons olive oil
- Salt and black pepper, to taste
- Fresh parsley, chopped, for garnish

Instructions:

Prepare Mushrooms:
- In a large skillet, heat 1 tablespoon of olive oil over medium heat.
- Add the sliced mushrooms and sauté until they are golden brown and any released liquid has evaporated. Set aside.

Start Risotto:
- In a separate large pan or Dutch oven, heat the remaining 1 tablespoon of olive oil over medium heat.
- Add the chopped onion and sauté until it becomes translucent.

Add Rice and Toast:
- Add Arborio rice to the pan, stirring to coat the rice with oil. Toast the rice for 1-2 minutes until the edges become translucent.

Deglaze with Brown Ale:
- Pour in the brown ale to deglaze the pan, stirring constantly until most of the liquid has been absorbed.

Begin Adding Broth:
- Start adding the warm chicken or vegetable broth, one ladle at a time, stirring continuously.
- Wait until the liquid is mostly absorbed before adding the next ladle of broth.

Continue Cooking:

- Continue this process until the rice is creamy and cooked to al dente texture. This usually takes about 18-20 minutes.

Add Mushrooms:
- Stir in the sautéed mushrooms during the last few minutes of cooking. Reserve a few for garnish if desired.

Finish with Butter and Cheese:
- Once the rice is cooked, remove the pan from heat.
- Stir in unsalted butter and grated Parmesan cheese until well combined.

Season and Garnish:
- Season the risotto with salt and black pepper according to your taste.
- Garnish with chopped fresh parsley and reserved sautéed mushrooms.

Serve Immediately:
- Serve the Brown Ale and Mushroom Risotto immediately, ensuring it is hot and creamy.

This Brown Ale and Mushroom Risotto is a comforting and indulgent dish, perfect for a cozy dinner. The brown ale adds a unique depth of flavor, and the combination of mushrooms, Parmesan, and Arborio rice creates a creamy and satisfying texture. Enjoy this delicious risotto as a main course or a side dish.

IPA Ceviche

Ingredients:

- 1 pound fresh white fish fillets (such as tilapia, snapper, or halibut), diced into small pieces
- 1 cup fresh lime juice (about 6-8 limes)
- 1 cup IPA beer
- 1 cup cherry tomatoes, halved
- 1/2 cup red onion, finely chopped
- 1/2 cup cucumber, diced
- 1/4 cup fresh cilantro, chopped
- 1 jalapeño, seeds removed and finely chopped
- 1 avocado, diced
- Salt and black pepper, to taste
- Tortilla chips, for serving

Instructions:

Prepare the Fish:
- In a non-reactive bowl, combine the diced fish with fresh lime juice. Make sure the fish is fully submerged in the lime juice. Cover the bowl and refrigerate for at least 30 minutes to "cook" the fish in the acidity of the lime juice. The fish should turn opaque when ready.

Drain Excess Lime Juice:
- After the fish has marinated, drain off excess lime juice. The lime juice will still contribute to the overall flavor, but you don't want the ceviche to be too watery.

Add IPA Beer:
- Pour the IPA beer over the marinated fish. The beer will add depth of flavor and complement the citrusy notes from the lime juice.

Combine Vegetables:
- Add halved cherry tomatoes, finely chopped red onion, diced cucumber, chopped cilantro, and finely chopped jalapeño to the fish and beer mixture.

Gently Mix:
- Gently toss the ingredients together until well combined. Be careful not to break the fish pieces.

Chill:

- Cover the ceviche and refrigerate for an additional 30 minutes to allow the flavors to meld.

Add Avocado:
- Right before serving, fold in diced avocado to the ceviche.

Season:
- Season the IPA Ceviche with salt and black pepper according to your taste.

Serve:
- Serve the IPA Ceviche chilled in individual bowls or glasses.
- Accompany with tortilla chips for scooping.

Enjoy:
- Enjoy the fresh and flavorful IPA Ceviche!

This IPA Ceviche is perfect for summer gatherings or as a light and refreshing appetizer. The addition of IPA beer adds a unique twist to the traditional ceviche, providing depth and complexity to the dish. Serve it with tortilla chips for a delightful and satisfying snack.

Beer and Herb Marinated Grilled Vegetables

Ingredients:

- Assorted vegetables for grilling (such as bell peppers, zucchini, eggplant, cherry tomatoes, mushrooms, and red onions)
- 1/2 cup beer (choose a light and crisp beer)
- 1/4 cup olive oil
- 2 cloves garlic, minced
- 2 tablespoons fresh herbs (such as rosemary, thyme, or oregano), chopped
- Salt and black pepper, to taste
- Lemon wedges for serving

Instructions:

Prepare Vegetables:
- Wash, clean, and cut the vegetables into bite-sized pieces or slices suitable for grilling.

Prepare Marinade:
- In a bowl, whisk together beer, olive oil, minced garlic, chopped fresh herbs, salt, and black pepper. This will be the marinade for the vegetables.

Marinate Vegetables:
- Place the prepared vegetables in a large bowl or zip-top bag.
- Pour the beer and herb marinade over the vegetables, ensuring they are well coated.
- Let the vegetables marinate for at least 30 minutes, allowing the flavors to infuse.

Preheat the Grill:
- Preheat your grill to medium-high heat.

Grill the Vegetables:
- Thread the marinated vegetables onto skewers or place them directly on the grill grates.
- Grill the vegetables for about 10-15 minutes, turning occasionally, until they are tender and have a nice char.

Baste with Marinade:
- While grilling, brush the vegetables with the remaining marinade to keep them moist and add extra flavor.

Check for Doneness:

- Check for doneness by testing the tenderness of the vegetables with a fork. Cooking times may vary depending on the size and type of vegetables.

Serve:
- Once the vegetables are grilled to perfection, remove them from the grill.
- Serve the Beer and Herb Marinated Grilled Vegetables on a platter, and squeeze fresh lemon wedges over the top for an extra burst of flavor.

Enjoy:
- Enjoy these flavorful grilled vegetables as a side dish or as a main course alongside your favorite grilled meats.

This Beer and Herb Marinated Grilled Vegetables recipe is versatile and can be adapted to include your favorite vegetables and herbs. The beer adds a subtle depth of flavor, making these grilled vegetables a delicious and memorable addition to your summer meals.

Beer and Caramelized Onion Pizza

Ingredients:

For the Pizza Dough:

- 1 pound pizza dough (store-bought or homemade)
- Cornmeal or flour for dusting

For the Toppings:

- 2 tablespoons olive oil
- 2 large onions, thinly sliced
- 1/2 cup beer (choose a malty or amber ale)
- 1 tablespoon brown sugar
- Salt and black pepper, to taste
- 1 cup shredded mozzarella cheese
- 1/2 cup crumbled blue cheese or goat cheese
- Fresh thyme leaves, for garnish (optional)

For the Beer Glaze:

- 1/4 cup beer
- 2 tablespoons honey or maple syrup

Instructions:

Preheat the Oven:
- Preheat your oven to the highest temperature setting, typically around 475°F to 500°F (245°C to 260°C).

Caramelize Onions:
- In a large skillet, heat olive oil over medium-low heat.
- Add thinly sliced onions and cook slowly until they become soft and golden brown, about 20-25 minutes.
- Pour in beer, add brown sugar, and continue cooking until the onions are caramelized and most of the liquid has evaporated.
- Season with salt and black pepper to taste.

Prepare Pizza Dough:
- Roll out the pizza dough on a lightly floured surface or on cornmeal-dusted parchment paper to your desired thickness.

Assemble the Pizza:
- Transfer the rolled-out dough to a pizza stone or baking sheet.
- Spread the caramelized onions evenly over the dough.
- Sprinkle shredded mozzarella cheese over the onions.
- Dot the pizza with crumbled blue cheese or goat cheese.

Bake the Pizza:
- Place the pizza in the preheated oven and bake for 12-15 minutes or until the crust is golden and the cheese is melted and bubbly.

Make Beer Glaze:
- While the pizza is baking, prepare the beer glaze by combining beer and honey or maple syrup in a small saucepan. Simmer over low heat until slightly reduced.

Finish and Garnish:
- Once the pizza is out of the oven, drizzle the beer glaze over the top.
- Garnish with fresh thyme leaves if desired.

Slice and Serve:
- Let the Beer and Caramelized Onion Pizza cool for a few minutes before slicing.
- Serve hot and enjoy!

This Beer and Caramelized Onion Pizza offers a perfect balance of sweet and savory flavors, and the addition of beer adds depth to both the onions and the glaze. It's a fantastic choice for pizza night or when you want to impress with a unique and delicious homemade pizza.

Chocolate Stout Pudding

Ingredients:

- 1/2 cup unsweetened cocoa powder
- 1/4 cup cornstarch
- 1 cup granulated sugar
- 1/4 teaspoon salt
- 2 1/2 cups whole milk
- 1 cup stout beer (such as Guinness)
- 6 ounces high-quality dark chocolate, finely chopped
- 3 large egg yolks
- 2 tablespoons unsalted butter
- 1 teaspoon vanilla extract
- Whipped cream and chocolate shavings for garnish (optional)

Instructions:

Mix Dry Ingredients:
- In a medium-sized saucepan, whisk together the cocoa powder, cornstarch, sugar, and salt until well combined.

Combine Wet Ingredients:
- Gradually whisk in the whole milk and stout beer until the mixture is smooth and free of lumps.

Heat Mixture:
- Place the saucepan over medium heat and bring the mixture to a simmer, stirring constantly.

Add Chopped Chocolate:
- Once the mixture is simmering, remove it from heat and add the finely chopped dark chocolate. Stir until the chocolate is completely melted and the mixture is smooth.

Temper the Egg Yolks:
- In a separate bowl, whisk the egg yolks. Gradually add a small amount of the chocolate mixture to the egg yolks while whisking constantly. This helps to temper the eggs and prevent them from curdling when added to the hot mixture.

Combine Mixtures:

- Pour the tempered egg mixture back into the saucepan with the rest of the chocolate mixture, stirring continuously.

Cook Until Thickened:
- Place the saucepan back on the heat and cook the mixture over medium heat, stirring constantly, until it thickens to a pudding-like consistency. This usually takes about 5-7 minutes.

Add Butter and Vanilla:
- Remove the saucepan from the heat and stir in the unsalted butter and vanilla extract until well incorporated.

Strain (Optional):
- For an extra smooth texture, you can strain the pudding through a fine-mesh sieve to remove any lumps.

Chill:
- Transfer the pudding to serving dishes or a large bowl and cover with plastic wrap, making sure the wrap is directly touching the surface of the pudding to prevent a skin from forming.
- Refrigerate for at least 2 hours or until the pudding is chilled and set.

Garnish and Serve:
- Before serving, garnish with whipped cream and chocolate shavings if desired.

Enjoy:
- Serve the Chocolate Stout Pudding chilled and enjoy the rich and delightful flavors.

This Chocolate Stout Pudding is a perfect dessert for chocolate and beer lovers alike. The stout beer adds a unique depth to the chocolate, creating a luscious and flavorful pudding. It's an ideal treat for special occasions or whenever you crave a decadent and comforting dessert.

Beer and Lime Grilled Shrimp

Ingredients:

- 1 pound large shrimp, peeled and deveined
- 1/2 cup beer (choose a light and citrusy beer)
- Juice and zest of 2 limes
- 3 tablespoons olive oil
- 3 cloves garlic, minced
- 1 teaspoon chili powder
- 1 teaspoon cumin
- 1 teaspoon paprika
- Salt and black pepper, to taste
- Fresh cilantro, chopped, for garnish
- Lime wedges, for serving

Instructions:

Marinate the Shrimp:
- In a bowl, combine beer, lime juice, lime zest, olive oil, minced garlic, chili powder, cumin, paprika, salt, and black pepper. Mix well to create the marinade.
- Add the peeled and deveined shrimp to the marinade, ensuring they are well-coated.
- Cover the bowl and refrigerate for at least 30 minutes to allow the flavors to infuse.

Preheat the Grill:
- Preheat your grill to medium-high heat.

Skewer the Shrimp:
- Thread the marinated shrimp onto skewers, making sure to leave a little space between each shrimp.

Grill the Shrimp:
- Place the shrimp skewers on the preheated grill.
- Grill for 2-3 minutes per side or until the shrimp are opaque and have grill marks.

Baste with Marinade:
- While grilling, baste the shrimp with the remaining marinade to enhance the flavor and keep them moist.

Check for Doneness:
- Shrimp cook quickly, so be attentive. They are done when they turn pink and opaque throughout.

Garnish and Serve:
- Remove the shrimp skewers from the grill and place them on a serving platter.
- Garnish with chopped fresh cilantro and serve with lime wedges on the side.

Enjoy:
- Serve the Beer and Lime Grilled Shrimp hot and enjoy the delicious citrusy and beer-infused flavors.

This Beer and Lime Grilled Shrimp is a fantastic dish for summer barbecues or any outdoor gathering. The beer and lime marinade adds a refreshing and zesty kick to the shrimp, making it a delightful and flavorful option for seafood lovers. Serve the shrimp as an appetizer or as part of a main course.

Ale and Garlic Roasted Chicken

Ingredients:

- 1 whole chicken (about 4-5 pounds)
- Salt and black pepper, to taste
- 1 tablespoon olive oil
- 4 cloves garlic, minced
- 1 tablespoon fresh rosemary, chopped
- 1 tablespoon fresh thyme, chopped
- 1 cup ale or your favorite beer
- 1 lemon, sliced
- 1 onion, sliced
- 2 tablespoons unsalted butter, melted

Instructions:

Preheat the Oven:
- Preheat your oven to 375°F (190°C).

Prepare the Chicken:
- Rinse the whole chicken under cold water and pat it dry with paper towels.
- Season the chicken inside and out with salt and black pepper.

Herb and Garlic Rub:
- In a small bowl, mix together the olive oil, minced garlic, chopped rosemary, and chopped thyme to create a herb and garlic rub.

Rub the Chicken:
- Rub the herb and garlic mixture all over the chicken, ensuring it's well-coated with the flavorful mixture.

Truss the Chicken (Optional):
- Truss the chicken with kitchen twine to help it cook more evenly.

Prepare the Roasting Pan:
- Place the chicken in a roasting pan.
- Pour the ale or beer into the bottom of the pan.

Add Aromatics:
- Stuff the cavity of the chicken with lemon slices and onion slices.

Roast the Chicken:

- Roast the chicken in the preheated oven for approximately 1.5 to 2 hours, or until the internal temperature reaches 165°F (74°C) in the thickest part of the thigh.

Baste with Ale:
- Periodically baste the chicken with the ale from the bottom of the roasting pan to keep it moist and add flavor.

Melted Butter Glaze:
- In the last 30 minutes of roasting, brush the chicken with melted butter to give it a golden and crispy skin.

Check for Doneness:
- Ensure the chicken is fully cooked by checking the internal temperature. The juices should run clear, and the skin should be golden and crispy.

Rest and Carve:
- Allow the chicken to rest for 10-15 minutes before carving. This helps the juices redistribute throughout the meat.

Serve:
- Carve the Ale and Garlic Roasted Chicken and serve it with your favorite side dishes.

Enjoy the succulent and flavorful Ale and Garlic Roasted Chicken, which pairs perfectly with the aromatic herbs, garlic, and the subtle taste of ale. This dish is a delightful option for a comforting and hearty meal.

IPA Pineapple Salsa

Ingredients:

- 2 cups fresh pineapple, diced
- 1/2 cup red onion, finely chopped
- 1 jalapeño, seeds removed and finely chopped
- 1/4 cup fresh cilantro, chopped
- Juice of 2 limes
- Zest of 1 lime
- 1/2 cup IPA beer (choose a citrusy or hoppy IPA)
- Salt and black pepper, to taste

Instructions:

Prepare the Ingredients:
- Dice the fresh pineapple into small, bite-sized pieces.
- Finely chop the red onion, jalapeño (seeds removed for less heat), and fresh cilantro.

Combine Ingredients:
- In a bowl, combine the diced pineapple, chopped red onion, jalapeño, and cilantro.

Add Lime Zest and Juice:
- Zest one lime directly into the bowl and squeeze the juice of both limes over the ingredients.

Pour in IPA Beer:
- Pour the IPA beer over the pineapple mixture. The beer adds a hoppy and citrusy flavor to the salsa.

Mix Well:
- Gently toss the ingredients together until well combined. Ensure the beer is evenly distributed.

Season:
- Season the salsa with salt and black pepper to taste. Adjust the seasoning according to your preference.

Chill:
- Cover the bowl and refrigerate the IPA Pineapple Salsa for at least 30 minutes to allow the flavors to meld.

Serve:

- Serve the salsa chilled, either on its own as a refreshing dip or alongside grilled meats, tacos, fish, or as a topping for various dishes.

Enjoy:
- Enjoy the vibrant and tangy flavors of IPA Pineapple Salsa!

This IPA Pineapple Salsa is a versatile and delicious accompaniment that adds a tropical twist to your meals. The combination of fresh pineapple, hoppy IPA beer, and zesty lime creates a unique and flavorful salsa that can elevate the taste of many dishes. It's perfect for summer gatherings, barbecues, or anytime you want to add a burst of freshness to your plate.

Beer and Sage Butter Pasta

Ingredients:

- 8 ounces pasta of your choice (such as fettuccine, linguine, or pappardelle)
- 1/2 cup unsalted butter
- 1/4 cup beer (choose a light and malty beer)
- 2 cloves garlic, minced
- 8-10 fresh sage leaves, chopped
- Salt and black pepper, to taste
- Grated Parmesan cheese, for serving
- Crushed red pepper flakes, for optional heat
- Fresh parsley, chopped, for garnish

Instructions:

Cook the Pasta:
- Cook the pasta according to the package instructions until al dente. Reserve a cup of pasta cooking water before draining.

Prepare the Beer and Sage Butter:
- In a large skillet or pan, melt the unsalted butter over medium heat.

Infuse with Sage and Garlic:
- Add the minced garlic and chopped sage leaves to the melted butter. Cook for 1-2 minutes until the sage becomes fragrant and the garlic is softened.

Add Beer:
- Pour in the beer, stirring well to combine. Allow the mixture to simmer for 2-3 minutes to infuse the flavors.

Season:
- Season the beer and sage butter sauce with salt and black pepper to taste. If you like some heat, you can add crushed red pepper flakes at this stage.

Combine with Pasta:
- Add the cooked and drained pasta to the skillet. Toss the pasta in the beer and sage butter sauce until well coated.

Adjust Consistency:
- If the pasta seems dry, add a splash of the reserved pasta cooking water to achieve your desired consistency.

Serve:

- Plate the Beer and Sage Butter Pasta, and sprinkle grated Parmesan cheese over the top.

Garnish and Enjoy:
- Garnish with fresh parsley and additional black pepper if desired.
- Serve the pasta hot and enjoy the rich and flavorful combination of beer-infused butter and sage.

This Beer and Sage Butter Pasta is a quick and easy dish that doesn't compromise on taste. The beer adds a unique depth to the buttery sauce, and the aromatic sage complements the flavors perfectly. It's a delightful option for a comforting weeknight dinner or a special meal with a touch of sophistication.

Porter and Chocolate Mousse

Ingredients:

- 8 ounces high-quality dark chocolate, chopped
- 1/2 cup unsalted butter
- 1/2 cup porter beer
- 1/4 cup granulated sugar
- Pinch of salt
- 4 large eggs, separated
- 1 teaspoon vanilla extract
- Whipped cream, for garnish (optional)
- Chocolate shavings, for garnish (optional)

Instructions:

Melt Chocolate and Butter:
- In a heatproof bowl, combine the chopped dark chocolate and unsalted butter. Melt them together using a double boiler or by microwaving in short bursts, stirring until smooth.

Add Porter Beer:
- Pour in the porter beer into the melted chocolate and butter mixture. Stir until well combined.

Sweeten and Add Salt:
- Add granulated sugar and a pinch of salt to the chocolate mixture. Stir until the sugar is dissolved.

Temper Egg Yolks:
- Whisk the egg yolks in a separate bowl. Gradually add a small amount of the chocolate mixture to the egg yolks while whisking constantly. This tempers the eggs, preventing them from curdling.

Combine Mixtures:
- Pour the tempered egg yolk mixture back into the chocolate mixture, stirring until well combined.

Add Vanilla Extract:
- Stir in the vanilla extract to enhance the flavor.

Whip Egg Whites:
- In a clean, dry bowl, whip the egg whites until stiff peaks form.

Fold in Egg Whites:

- Gently fold the whipped egg whites into the chocolate mixture until no white streaks remain. Be careful not to deflate the egg whites.

Chill:
- Spoon the mousse into serving glasses or ramekins.
- Refrigerate the Porter and Chocolate Mousse for at least 4 hours or overnight to set.

Garnish and Serve:
- Before serving, garnish the mousse with whipped cream and chocolate shavings if desired.

Enjoy:
- Serve the Porter and Chocolate Mousse chilled and savor the luxurious combination of beer-infused chocolate goodness.

This Porter and Chocolate Mousse is a delightful treat for chocolate and beer enthusiasts. The porter beer adds a depth of flavor to the rich and velvety chocolate mousse, creating a dessert that's perfect for special occasions or when you want to indulge in something truly decadent.

Porter and Chocolate Mousse

Ingredients:

- 8 ounces high-quality dark chocolate, chopped
- 1/2 cup unsalted butter
- 1/2 cup porter beer
- 1/4 cup granulated sugar
- Pinch of salt
- 4 large eggs, separated
- 1 teaspoon vanilla extract
- Whipped cream, for garnish (optional)
- Chocolate shavings, for garnish (optional)

Instructions:

Melt Chocolate and Butter:
- In a heatproof bowl, combine the chopped dark chocolate and unsalted butter. Melt them together using a double boiler or by microwaving in short bursts, stirring until smooth.

Add Porter Beer:
- Pour in the porter beer into the melted chocolate and butter mixture. Stir until well combined.

Sweeten and Add Salt:
- Add granulated sugar and a pinch of salt to the chocolate mixture. Stir until the sugar is dissolved.

Temper Egg Yolks:
- Whisk the egg yolks in a separate bowl. Gradually add a small amount of the chocolate mixture to the egg yolks while whisking constantly. This tempers the eggs, preventing them from curdling.

Combine Mixtures:
- Pour the tempered egg yolk mixture back into the chocolate mixture, stirring until well combined.

Add Vanilla Extract:
- Stir in the vanilla extract to enhance the flavor.

Whip Egg Whites:
- In a clean, dry bowl, whip the egg whites until stiff peaks form.

Fold in Egg Whites:

- Gently fold the whipped egg whites into the chocolate mixture until no white streaks remain. Be careful not to deflate the egg whites.

Chill:
- Spoon the mousse into serving glasses or ramekins.
- Refrigerate the Porter and Chocolate Mousse for at least 4 hours or overnight to set.

Garnish and Serve:
- Before serving, garnish the mousse with whipped cream and chocolate shavings if desired.

Enjoy:
- Serve the Porter and Chocolate Mousse chilled and savor the luxurious combination of beer-infused chocolate goodness.

This Porter and Chocolate Mousse is a delightful treat for chocolate and beer enthusiasts. The porter beer adds a depth of flavor to the rich and velvety chocolate mousse, creating a dessert that's perfect for special occasions or when you want to indulge in something truly decadent.